Hey Ari,

I thought this looked interesting. I hope you like it.

Lots of Love
David

TORN
BETWEEN
TWO
CULTURES

A Capital Currents Book, a category that offers an insider's look at topics of concern today. Other titles include:

The $100,000 Teacher: A Teacher's Solution to America's Declining Public School System by Brian Crosby

The Other Side of Welfare: Real Stories from a Single Mother by Pamela L. Cave

David, Goliath, and the Beach-Cleaning Machine: How a Small California Town Fought an Oil Giant and Won by Barbara M. Wolcott

TORN BETWEEN TWO CULTURES

An Afghan-American Woman Speaks Out

MARYAM QUDRAT ASEEL

A Capital Currents Book

CAPITAL
BOOKS, INC.
Sterling, Virginia

Capital Books, Inc.
P.O. Box 605
Herndon, Virginia 20172-0605

Photo of mosque on front cover by Douglas R. Powell.
Photo of author on front cover by Photo Prestige of Beverly Hills.
Photos of wedding by Photo Prestige of Beverly Hills.

ISBN 1-931868-36-0 (alk.paper)

Library of Congress Cataloging-in-Publication Data

Aseel, Maryam Qudrat, 1974–
    Torn between two cultures : an Afghan-American woman speaks out / Maryam Qudrat. — 1st ed.
        p.   cm. — (A Capital currents book)
    Includes bibliographical references and index.
    ISBN 1-931868-36-0
    1. Aseel, Maryam Qudrat, 1974–   2. Afghan American women — Biography.   3. Afghan Americans — Biography.   4. Muslims — United States — Biography.   5. Afghan Americans — Ethnic identity.   6. United States — Relations — Afghanistan.   7. Afghanistan — Relations — United States.   8. East and West.   I. Title.   II. Series.
    E184.A23A84   2003
    305.48′891593073′092 — dc21   2002041108

Printed in the United States of America on acid-free paper that meets the American National Standards Institute Z39-48 Standard.

First Edition

10   9   8   7   6   5   4   3   2

*I dedicate this book, for the sake of God,
to the pursuit of truth and understanding
among the peoples of the East
and the West.*

CONTENTS

Acknowledgments   ix

Author's Note   xi

Prologue   xiii

1 A Dark Summer in Afghanistan   1

2 Afghans in America   25

3 Coming Together, Falling Apart   45

4 Growing Up Muslim Afghan-American   65

5 Revisiting Afghanistan   93

6 Womanhood   117

7 The Real Islam   141

8 Between Old Friends   165

9 As the Smoke Clears   177

Epilogue   187

Index   189

ACKNOWLEDGMENTS

I am indebted to Mr. Kubelka, the true source of inspiration for this book; to Tracey Creech, for her tireless work and patience with draft after draft of late-night edits and invaluable critiques and suggestions; and to Dr. John Dreher, for his support and committed role in my intellectual and philosophical growth.

I thank my husband, Samir Aseel, for his continued support in this as well as all endeavors. You are a source of encouragement, happiness, and peace in a world full of difficulty and chaos. For that I am grateful every day of my life.

I thank my parents, Abdul Qadeer and Shaesta Qudrat, for giving me strength and dismissing my tantrums in the midst of this and all other projects I tackle. You are the apple of my eye; I love you to a measure that no words can explain or actions can show. I only hope that my accomplishments bring you the pleasure that you rightfully deserve and that you have worked so hard to earn now and always.

Thanks to my father-in-law, the charismatic Mr. Ayub Assil, for spending so much time patiently combing through my manuscript. You are one of a kind, and you treat me like a princess in a fairy tale. I appreciate all that you do and say and love you dearly.

Thanks to Haseena, my one and only sister, for her strong criticisms and dedication throughout the process of writing. Thank you for your prayers, love, kindness, and loyalty—I am truly blessed.

Finally, thanks to my not-so-little brother, Omar, who takes my criticisms so well. You are the next Plato of our time. You mean everything to me.

AUTHOR'S NOTE

Observant Muslims show respect for the Prophet Muhammad (peace be upon him), as well as other acknowledged prophets such as Abraham, Moses, or Jesus (peace be upon them), by saying "peace be upon him" after speaking their names. Similarly, the abbreviation "pbuh" is used after their names in written text. I have followed that tradition in this book.

※ ※

Lagabs are "substitute names" used by Afghans to show respect in addressing another person. Examples are *Koh Koh Jan* for my grandmother and *Khan Kaka* for Uncle Khalil. *Jan* is a term of endearment.

※ ※

The names of some of the people whose personal stories I relate in this book have been changed to protect their identities.

PROLOGUE

I am an Afghan-American woman, born in Los Angeles in 1974 to Afghans who immigrated before all hell broke loose in their homeland. The Soviet aggression that prevented my parents from returning to Afghanistan for more than twenty years has afforded me the opportunity to speak today, without visceral anger toward the Taliban and without animosity toward the United States, to anyone who will listen.

I have lived an Afghan-American life, a hyphenated life that does not fit fully into any social category; deeply embedded in me lie two value systems that have grown to signify polar extremes, those of the East and West. In *me* they have come to exist peacefully, yet outside of me they are at war . . . or are they? I wonder, are the ideologies and practices of the East and West actually at war, or is it just that ignorance, shallow judgment, and apathy have gripped our hearts?

Another gross act of aggression, the attacks of September 11, set the East and West on a collision course. We turn to each other for a solution, an answer. Yet all that emerges as an answer is more violence and war. I watch the destruction that continues to escalate and know that it will lead us exactly to the point of no return. There is only so much blood that can be shed, only so much vengeance that can be exacted. At some point the knife will be pushed in so deep that we will not be able to extract it and retreat from what we have done.

I find my life and my self straddling the gulf between these civilizations of the East and West. Through a lifetime of introspection and struggle, I have been able to work through the stigmas and misconceptions to reconcile them within me. My own life is testimony to the fact that the ideologies of the East and West are not truly at war—only their people are. And these people are at war because they don't know each other. If they don't know each other, how can they understand each other?

As I write, I realize the risks involved in what I say, for I am now considered to be a questionable member of society by virtue of my heritage and religion. I cannot claim to have the same civil liberties I used to have, liberties that everyone else stakes claim to. I encompass the identity of an Afghan as well as of a Muslim. This is considered a dangerous combination where I live, because people do not know what it means.

To begin to understand, we must see the whole picture, how we got here, and how things got so far beyond our control without our even realizing it. We must examine the roots of our relationship. Only then can we begin anew. An honest and accurate analysis of our history allows us to learn from past experience so that we might improve present and future conditions, whereas self-censorship can only defeat all of us—Afghans, Muslims, and Americans (and all the combinations thereof) alike. We simply cannot afford to repeat the mistakes of the past. We must look to the past as a point of reference so that we can better formulate the direction in which we want Afghanistan and its allies to go in the future. Certainly this is the purpose of revisiting history.

We have our guns pointed at each other, when in fact the enemy is ignorance and apathy. Such an enemy cannot be destroyed with guns, planes, bombs, or suicide. It is an inferno that can be extinguished with human understanding, for which there is no substitute.

Many of the opinions and perspectives that I will share with you are those of the Afghan Muslim community. What exactly is this "Afghan community"? Today approximately seven million Afghans live outside Afghanistan, making them the largest group of refugees in the world. The vast majority of these Afghans left their country during the last twenty-four years of war and strife. I live in Southern California, along with thousands of other Afghans. Yet though we are many and spread far and wide, our community is very tightly knit. Afghans know one another through family names, and they have ways of finding out more about those whom they don't know yet. A family's entire history can be discovered through a few phone calls.

When you are in touch with the Afghan community, it is an easy thing to discover the "buzz," the general direction of opinion. For while Afghans are diverse in many ways and hold many different viewpoints, we agree on certain basic principles. The views of Afghans that I relate in this book are based on speaking to people in the Afghan community as well as being in tune with the "buzz." Naturally I can't speak for everyone, but I attempt to give an idea of the consensus of the mainstream Afghan majority.

And so I invite you on a journey into my religion, my culture, and my community, to meet some of my fellow countrymen and to get a clear firsthand view behind the mystery of what lies on the other side of the world. This is not a Western commentator's account of Afghans, Islam, and the Taliban. It is my Afghan-American voice, from within the Muslim mind, that speaks directly to you.

In this book I seek to share a bit of myself and tell how the East and West have grown to coexist in the microcosm of my life, in hopes that it will not fall on deaf ears. And I aspire to restore the belief that we are all just people, not as different as we seem, and certainly closer than we appear.

TIMELINE: MODERN HISTORY OF AFGHANISTAN

1919   Under King Amanullah Shah, Afghanistan defeats would-be British colonizers in the third and final Anglo-Afghan war. The king declares the country's full independence.

1929   General Mohammad Nadir Khan overthrows a usurper and assumes kingship.

1933   King Nadir Shah is assassinated; his young son, Zahir Shah, becomes king. During Zahir Shah's rule, economic and social reforms continue, a constitutional monarchy providing for elections and a free press is introduced, and women become increasingly active in education, business, and politics.

1973   Zahir Shah's cousin, Mohammad Daoud, seizes power, declares Afghanistan a republic, and names himself president. Zahir Shah goes into exile in Rome.

1978   Afghan communists backed by the Soviet Union assassinate Daoud. Noor Taraki becomes president. Five months later, Taraki is assassinated and Hafizullah Amin assumes power.

1979   In December, Soviet forces invade Afghanistan, assassinate Amin, and install Babrak Karmal as leader.

1980s   United States (under the Reagan administration) supplies weapons and training to Afghan mujahideen resistance to fight Soviet aggression.

1989   The Soviet army withdraws from Afghanistan in defeat. In November, the Berlin Wall falls, signifying the end of the Cold War. Afghans divide into factions and civil war begins.

1991   Soviet Union collapses. United States begins rolling back aid to Afghanistan.

1992   Afghan factions are strategically supported by various countries, giving them a stronghold and further fueling the civil war.

1994   Taliban takes control of Kandahar.

1996   Taliban takes control of Kabul and establishes rule over Afghanistan, except for those areas controlled by the Northern Alliance.

2001   *September 9*: The leader of the Northern Alliance, Ahmad Shah Masoud, is assassinated.
        September 11: Terrorists attack U.S. targets in a coordinated effort.
        October: United States begins air strikes in Afghanistan.
        November: Taliban abandons Kabul.
        December: Taliban abandons Kandahar. Hamid Karzai is sworn in as interim leader of Afghanistan.

2002   Former king Zahir Shah returns from exile in Rome. Hamid Karzai is elected president of Afghanistan.

2004   Democratic presidential elections scheduled to convene in Afghanistan.

✑ One ✑

A Dark Summer in Afghanistan

When I was a young girl in the 1980s, I watched my small family unit grow exponentially as our refugee relations poured into the United States. I was astounded every time we went to the airport to pick up the next group of new arrivals. To meet cousins, aunts, and uncles who were so warm and loving upon seeing me was incredible—I had been so young when I had first met them in Afghanistan, and my memories were faint.

My grandmother, Koh Koh Jan, was especially pleased to see me again, and delighted to meet my little sister and brother for the first time. She lovingly told me that the reason I was named Maryam was because she had told my dad, "If you ever have a daughter, I want you to name her after my mother." Her mother had died in her twenties, ostensibly from a "rare illness" that was not properly diagnosed. She hoped that the memory of her mother's short life could live on through me.

My relatives were full of stories, which they told every time the family got together. Every so often they would ask, "Do you remember the time when . . . ?" As I listened, these tales of a distant land began to touch a familiar place in my mind. My memories awakened from their deep sleep. It was not long before I could vividly recall the most dramatic and traumatic details of my one trip to Afghanistan.

❧ ☙

It was spring of 1978, and still beautiful and warm in downtown Kabul when my mom and I finished shopping in the bazaar. I remember distinctly how the sun shone into my eyes as we sat in the back of the taxi. My mother, Shaesta held my hand tightly as I fidgeted in the seat, eager to show my grandparents and cousins all the wonderful gifts we had bought. The taxi driver was stereotypically reckless as he swerved from our side of the road into the lane of oncoming traffic and back. My mother yelled at him to watch the road. He brusquely retorted, *"Hamshira, sister, how would you know anything about driving?"*

My mom and I looked at each other, then broke into chuckles. What would this smug man's reaction be if he could see her nimbly navigating the massive loops and knots of metropolitan freeways as she did every day back home? My mom's two girlfriends, sitting in the front seat, looked back at us and giggled too.

The four of us had set out that morning on a mission to find Afghan specialty items and souvenirs for my dad, who had stayed in Los Angeles for this trip. I was very upset that he hadn't come with us, but I was just four years old and didn't have much say in the matter. Soon we would discover that his decision to stay home was one of the most fortunate accidents of our lives.

❧ ☙

My mom had been friends with our two shopping companions since their college days at Kabul University. These women were not married, nor did they wish to be. They enjoyed their independence and felt no need to be tied down. Actually, none of my mom's close friends were married. These Kabuli women didn't need husbands to support them or buy their dignity for them. Their opinion was, if marriage happened, it happened. If it didn't, they didn't fear the consequences; after all, they had good educations and financial freedom. Education, money, and gainful employment were not impossible for a woman to achieve on her own. By and large, they controlled their own lives.

My mom's friends were fashionably chic, which was also common among the young women of Kabul. I admired their stylish skirt-suits and dresses and fancy high-heeled shoes. Afghan women could dress as they pleased. Some chose to dress in burqas or other traditional attire, wearing loose pants to cover their legs under their conservative skirts and winding light, sheer *gach* scarves around their hair. Others dressed in miniskirts that were pretty darned mini.

Modern fashion was common at Kabul University, where most students dressed in style. Guys came to class in suits and ties, or at least in dress shirts and slacks. Girls wore the latest Western fashions, which included the aforementioned miniskirts along with platform shoes and frosty pink lipstick and nail polish. Through fashion, these young men and women celebrated the freedom of finally being able to commingle in the classroom, for before college their classrooms had been separated by gender, and the wearing of uniforms had been strictly enforced. This was an exciting time in their lives.

My cousin Laila was one of these lucky college students. She was tall and French-looking, and was considered to be the prettiest girl in our family. But being single, stylish, and popular wasn't all easy. Her door was always thronged by suitors asking for her hand in marriage. It was quite a burden for her to deal with after a long day of meeting the demands of the university, where standards and expectations were quite high. If Laila or her fellow classmates were to fail an important test such as a final exam, they would fail the entire course. And if they failed a course, they could not make up that single class—rather, they would be held back an entire year to retake every class in the grade level. Students were under tremendous pressure to succeed, to avoid the humiliation of watching their classmates move on to the next level while they were left behind. Some of my other relatives still wake up in cold sweats from nightmares about going to class to take an exam that they are not prepared for. Luckily, Laila was at the top of her class and was eventually offered a scholarship to study in Switzerland, which she accepted.

In the capital of Afghanistan, education was highly esteemed. Among those Afghans who had the opportunity to get an education in any field, it was absolutely expected that they do so. If a young person decided not to go to college after high school, he or she was judged severely, especially the men. If a man approached a woman's family to make a marriage proposal and did not have a degree, he stood almost no chance of being accepted.

Traditionally, men were the breadwinners and women were the caretakers. This meant that Afghan women did not have the same pressure to further their higher education as men, as it was expected that they would eventually rely upon the support of their husbands. However, this did not stop women such as my mom, Laila, and all of their friends from going to college. In fact, girls who did not pursue their college studies were naturally eliminated from their social circle, since they were no longer sharing the same goals or spending as much time together. The time spent at university also made it a natural place for young Afghans to meet their future spouses.

It was at the university that my mom and dad first met. It was a union that almost didn't happen. Shortly after my mom met him, the university awarded her a scholarship to study in the field of education in the Soviet Union. She actually wanted to study law, and refused the scholarship to Russia, instead deciding to head to America to complete her baccalaureate degree. To avoid the heartbreak of saying good-bye, she decided to leave without telling my dad. But at the end of a typing class, my dad's friend overheard her talking to the professor about how she was leaving Afghanistan and needed to arrange to exit the class early. The friend relayed this to my dad, who promptly followed her to California. They married soon after in the lovely oceanside town of Pacific Palisades.

Usually Afghan daughters live with their parents and are married at their parents' discretion, in the manner their parents want. So it was somewhat untraditional that my mom's parents flew halfway across the world to attend the wedding ceremony. However, they didn't operate under traditional precepts.

Their primary concern was for their children's happiness, and they didn't impose their will upon them. They didn't require that their children marry only people from a certain part of the country. They didn't even require that their children's spouses be from Afghanistan. Whether they spoke Pashto or Farsi was not an issue—although, to be sure, my grandfather did enjoy conversing in Pashto with his one Pashto-speaking son-in-law. In short, when it came to their children's aspirations, they were open-minded and unselfish. They lived in Kabul, which was one of the most developed areas in Afghanistan, with all the kinds of buildings and facilities that one is accustomed to seeing in Western countries. They were both educated and had been privileged with many opportunities. My grandmother had been principal of an all-girls' school. My grandfather, a great patriot, was renowned for being Afghanistan's very first air force pilot.

My dad's family didn't come to the wedding—because my dad chose not to tell them about it. His family was very traditional. He knew they wouldn't take kindly to him simply announcing his wedding. He was supposed to ask permission in the manner that was appropriate for his family. Courtship and marriage were to take place at their discretion, not his own. His mother, Koh Koh Jan, had single-handedly arranged the marriages of three of her children. By not telling his family about the wedding, my dad managed to circumvent the issue of tradition altogether. It was only after I was born that he wrote them a letter to tell them what had transpired and sent them pictures of his new family.

Kabulis, who generally were more liberal, Westernized, and progressive, represented a very small slice of the country in number and in character. They usually had more education and, consequently, the opportunity to get better jobs, make higher wages, and experience the world outside of Afghanistan. The great majority of Afghans lived in rural areas and remained closely tied to their own cultural value systems. This is the system that my dad's parents lived by, and the prospect of persuading his parents to bend their lifelong beliefs, particularly about something as important as marriage, was not good.

My parents' wedding took place at a time when Afghan citizens were free to roam the world at their leisure, so my mom's parents had no problem making the trip. After they arrived in the U.S., my mom and other relatives tried to convince them to stay permanently. My grandmother was game because she wanted to live near her children, most of whom had relocated to the United States. But my grandfather refused. He felt indebted to his country for his success and for the successes of his children. He also believed that the respect and dignity he commanded in his own country would be lost if he moved to America. At home, he was highly esteemed; here, he would be just another old immigrant, struggling to communicate and interact with a new culture. So after the wedding, my grandparents returned to Afghanistan. The next time they would see my mother was during our trip in 1978.

❦ ❦

I wasn't accustomed to Afghan cuisine prior to this trip, because my mom didn't cook Afghan food in the first years of her marriage. Back home in the U.S., the basmati rices that were so essential to good Afghan cooking were not yet readily available. She also wanted to avoid those heavy foods in the interest of her figure. Afghani dishes consist primarily of rice and meat, but Afghans have managed to transform regular white rice into the basis of a bounty of delectable recipes—for example, emerald rice, which is cooked and then baked in spinach, and *qabili*, rice baked in chicken broth and sprinkled with sliced carrots and raisins. When my dad discovered Uncle Ben's instant rice he was over-whelmed with joy, he had so missed the presence of rice in his life.

To celebrate our arrival in Afghanistan, my mom's family cooked up a storm — a colorful variety of exquisite, flavorful dishes made with farm-fresh, organically grown ingredients. Yet the Af-ghan meal I discovered I loved best was baked bread and water. It sounds like a dry and tasteless combination, but in Afghanistan they tasted so good and refreshing to me. This odd preference con-cerned my cousin Laila. Once, when she returned home from the university, she asked me what I had eaten that day. Of course, I proudly told her, "bread and water." She felt very sorry for me, and promptly went out to take two buses to an exclusive grocery store called Aziz Supermarket, where she bought me what she felt was more appetizing food: Swiss chocolate, crackers, cream cheese, cereal, and other specialty fare that only Aziz Supermarket carried.

At one point during our trip, I asked my mom if we could go home real quick to pick up some ravioli and pizza. She patiently explained to me that we were too far away to be able to do that. Her response was yet more evidence for my hunch that we were in some kind of time-travel situation. For even though Kabul was modern in many ways, there was an ancient quality to many of its sights and sounds that reminded me of fairy tales from long ago. I felt light years from Los Angeles.

~≈ ≈~

Now that we were in Afghanistan, my mother would finally have to meet my father's side of the family. She was under a lot of pressure. Considering the circumstances of the marriage, her new in-laws might not be happy with her. And because they were very traditional, she would have to be especially conscious of her man-ners and how she chose her topics of conversation.

She need not have worried. The family awaited our arrival eagerly. They too prepared a great feast for us, and were nothing but welcoming and hospitable. It turned out that they already knew my mother's family—when they had first heard about the marriage, they visited them to pay their respects, and had been making efforts to include them in their social functions ever since. So by the time my mom and I first met my dad's family, all of our relatives were well acquainted.

Although my dad's parents lived in Kabul, their values were relatively traditional. His mother was one of many women who continued to dress in traditional attire even though the state no longer required it. Koh Koh Jan was of Sayed lineage, which means she was directly descended from the Prophet Muhammad (pbuh). She was born in Herat, the cultural heart of the country in terms of poetry, art, comedy, and architectural achievements such as the gorgeous mosque of Masjid Jama'a Herat. She was beautiful and very strong, and took charge of the lives of her sons and their wives and children. She had all of their homes built on a single strip of land, with her own home in the very center and paths leading from their homes to hers. Her home was the sun, and my uncles' homes were the planets that revolved around it. The only ones who managed to escape her gravity were my father, who had gone to America, and my uncle Khan Kaka, who had slipped away to Canada. ("Kaka" means uncle in Dari.)

Even when my uncles were married, she did not treat them like independent adults. She implemented her own decisions and opinions on how things should be handled, whether they liked it or not. She justified this behavior as most parents do: she was doing it for their own good. She did not feel that their ages mattered in her right to make decisions for them. She was very loving and affectionate while entirely temperamental.

The people of her hometown of Herat held onto many of the traditional opinions that people in the city of Kabul had abandoned as obsolete. Yet though my grandmother wore a burqa, she was by no means a subservient woman. Ironically, the burqa was seen as more of a fashion statement, and fashion was dictated from the city and emulated from that point of reference just as it trickles from L.A., New York, and other major cities here in the States. As a product of her era, she did feel that girls should be well versed in the arts of cooking, sewing, and other domestic activities, and didn't think school was a priority. She had been taught by her elders that if girls are taught to read and write too well, the next thing you know they will be writing love letters to boys. She believed that girls should learn their alphabet only enough to be able to sound out the Arabic words of the Quran so that they could read it. Interestingly, her only daughter became a teacher; I don't know how she managed to get that by my grandmother.

Her husband, my grandfather, was of Mohammadzai lineage (yahyakhail). He was born in the Pashto-speaking areas of Laghman, but his family was from the Helmand Valley of Kandahar. His family is renowned for having held the famous Koohi-Noor ("mountain of light") diamond. This spectacular jewel, which is now over 100 carats after having been cut down many times, had been given as a gift in the 1700s by Nadir (Afshar) Shah of Persia, who obtained it from the spoils of war when he invaded India, to his general Ahmad Shah Baba. Ahmad Shah Baba later became the king of Afghanistan and gave it to one of his generals, my great-great-grandfather Sardar Sultan Mohammad Khan, who was also known as Telayee. ("Telayee" means "golden," referring to the gold plates and utensils that he insisted on eating from.) The diamond was passed down from son to son until eventually it was sold in India by my late great-grandfather's wife. When India was annexed by the British, the East India Company obtained it and in 1850 presented it to Queen Victoria, who displayed it at the Crystal Palace Exposition. The diamond is now displayed among the British crown jewels at the Tower of London.

My grandfather was a disciplinarian. None of his children had the nerve even to start a conversation with him. They addressed him only as "sir." He was a military man with a militaristic parenting style. But he also had his favorites—naturally, the tougher children, including my Canadian uncle, who inherited the mix of my grandmother's affectionate nature and hot temper.

Meeting my dad's family was very pleasant for me. My many new cousins were intrigued that I had come from America and were wary of me at first, but before long they were teaching me a nursery-rhyme song in Pashto: *"Damangi gharayi shna laman speena kana. . . ."* We sang this song as we played the new games that they taught me. In one, you held hands with your partner, crossing one arm over the other and leaning backward as you simultaneously twirled in a circle. Whoever got dizziest first would drop out and lose the game. My youngest uncle, Shair Kaka, joined in the fun, chasing me around the yard on his roller skates and then making up for it by taking us out for ice cream.

As we played, I noticed an older woman smoking a kind of pipe that was attached to a large decorative holder. I had never seen a hookah or chelam pipe before. It scared me a little. It made strange gurgling sounds as the woman inhaled the smoke of the *shisha*, tobacco ground up with fruit molasses. It looked very dangerous. At my age, I had no idea that such pipes could be found all over Los Angeles, particularly in the college town of Westwood where I was born.

When Afghans travel to far-off places, they do not customarily arrive empty-handed. We arrived in Afghanistan with six suitcases full of gifts for family and friends. Our personal luggage amounted to only two suitcases for what was intended to be a three-month-long vacation. Among the most essential American items we brought were cartons of Pop Rocks candy. My mom hadn't told me that these were packed in our suitcases for fear that I would devour them before we got off the plane. When she finally produced them, she told the unsuspecting Afghans that she had brought a very tasty candy from America, in fact the most popular candy in the States. Afghans were accustomed to candy, but the tales of it being a hot American product made it much more enticing. Then she poured handfuls of Pop Rocks into their mouths. Their amazed reactions to the taste and feel of the crackling candy as it made contact with their tongues were hysterically funny. I wondered if some of them might get angry that we got such a kick out of their naivete, but they knew it was all in good fun.

Luckily, our emptied suitcases could be used to bring home all kinds of Afghan goods: traditional dresses, rugs, lapis jewelry, decorative tapestries, and various trinkets. These items were colorful and artistic, rich in ornate and intricate designs. I especially loved the brightly colored gowns that were worn with the traditional *tomban*, parachute-style pants of contrasting color. The dresses' midsections, which covered the chest area down to the waistline, were often adorned with small round mirrors, beautiful embroidery, and colorful woven brocade. Decorative silver jewelry hung from the shoulders and waist. The outfits were so much fun to wear, especially with sheer matching scarves laced in gorgeous beadwork. I felt like a grown-up lady when I wore my Afghan dress, and I even managed to convince my mom to let me wear high-heeled shoes with it. What a treat!

We bought Afghan rugs in hues of deep burgundy and red, with geometric designs such as connecting rows of pentagons and octagons. Besides being beautiful, the rugs were of exceptional quality, made to last through many decades of wear and tear. It was a puzzle to figure out how we would lug those rugs home. We decided that we would roll them up in long cardboard containers and carry them on the plane ourselves.

We also bought tapestries and jewelry. Lapis is a common stone in Afghanistan, often used in making silver jewelry. The settings were decorative, with dangling strands of lapis cut into teardrop shapes. I opted for a silver hair ornament to be set on my bangs toward the middle of my forehead, in front of my sheer matching scarf. This jewelry was heavy with precious metals and stones, but the prices we paid for everything we bought seemed very reasonable. One U.S. dollar converted to about eighty Afghanis. A decent seat for a movie cost around fifteen Afghanis. An egg cost one or two Afghanis, far less than its 2001 price of more than forty thousand Afghanis. With our American dollars, we were able to spend quite liberally.

~& 9~

The Kabul bazaar that we visited that warm April day was not like the farmer's markets that I knew from home, though it did include the same hustle and bustle of people bargaining with merchants and pushing through crowds to gather their merchandise. The ground wasn't paved, so dust clouds and dirt flew all about. The road in front of my grandparents' house was also unpaved, so I faced these dust attacks every time I went out the door. My eyes got so irritated that sometimes I just kept them shut and held someone's hand to lead me.

The experience of the bazaar was well worth this nuisance. We took along beautiful velvet brocade bags in which to carry our merchandise — so different from home, where we were handed our purchases in plastic or paper bags. I was exhilarated after these outings, seeing the diverse crowd of people speaking different languages, dressed in all kinds of styles. Some traditional women wore long, flowing, fashionable burqas that covered them from head to toe, with holes poked out of the sheetlike material to see through. The burqas were richly colored, some in deep burgundies and other royal-colored hues, and decorated with carefully hand-stitched embroidery. Some women wore small Afghani hats underneath their burqas to heighten the fashion statement. Other Kabuli women showed up in Western high fashion. Some men arrived at the bazaar in traditional garb, a kind of gown that extended below the knees, and matching parachute pants. Their bodices were decorated with intricate embroidery, usually in white. Some men speaking Pashto wore turbans or traditional hats, while others speaking Farsi or other languages dressed in typical Western attire.

I later learned that in Kabul, Farsi—or, more accurately, Dari—was the primary language spoken. Farsi, which is spoken by Iranians, differs from Dari in that Farsi has been influenced by Arabic and French; Dari is considered to be more "pure." The difference between Farsi and Dari to those who understand the languages might be compared to the difference between Shakespearean and modern English. Interestingly enough, Afghans tend to be able to understand Farsi-speaking Iranians with no problem, but Iranians often find it hard to decipher what Afghans are talking about.

At the bazaar I was particularly struck by the diversity of people's physical appearance. Some looked European or American, with blonde hair and blue eyes, while others had darker complexions, looking more like Indians or Pakistanis. But I was most surprised when I encountered Afghans who looked like my conception of someone from East Asia. These Afghans had almond-shaped eyes and flat facial features. It was odd to see Afghans looking so different from one another. They behaved similarly and seemed to commingle without any sense of hostility or tension. They just looked different.

Customer service in the bazaar was different from what I knew at home. In the U.S., the customer was always right. Here, the merchants were in full command. I watched as one customer pushed a merchant a bit too far with her haggling efforts, after which point the merchant refused to sell to her. She immediately agreed to his price, but he politely told her that the item was not for sale anymore, and neither was anything else in his store. These business owners were not wealthy, but they cultivated a self-important demeanor, conscious of the fact that they possessed something that shoppers wanted. They refused to beg for a sale or cave in to the demands of customers.

The bazaar emphasized the differences between Afghan and American cultures. Afghan people tended to be very friendly, and strangers spoke with one another almost as though they knew each other. There was a lack of formality in the bazaars and in other public places; I heard people make comments that I had thought were appropriate only for those with whom one was familiar. When we were indecisive about a purchase, merchants told us firmly what was obviously the right choice, and that was not necessarily the item that would turn the biggest profit. People from the street—cab drivers, store clerks, and anyone else who felt like it—came right up to me and pinched my cheeks (and quite hard, I might add). I had never experienced total strangers approaching me like this, especially so forcefully.

Sometimes I saw public fights, especially on the overcrowded buses. People would start arguing about nonsensical things, probably because they were so cramped. There was no maximum occupancy on the bus; anybody could board as long as they could find a space to hang on. Their conception of personal space was different from mine. They were comfortable well inside the arm's-length radius that I considered a normal distance from people I didn't know.

While all of these sights and sounds had me awestruck, the real highlight of the bazaar for me was the animals. At home we had to travel long distances to see wild animals or even common livestock such as horses, cows, and sheep. Even then they were at a zoo or farm, far from reach and usually in cages. Here at the bazaar, it overwhelmed me to see flocks of animals crossing the street in such a nonchalant manner. Some people attended to whole caravans of animals in plain view of everyone.

Afghans tend to view animals as dirty, lowly beings that exist to serve some practical purpose, such as guarding their homes, keeping them warm with pelts, or providing them food. Nobody wanted to pet these animals or showed any interest in them at all—well, nobody except for *this* Afghan girl. I was absolutely overcome with excitement when I saw these wonderful creatures. I could stop and pet them as I pleased without worrying about any "Do not touch or feed the animals" signs. I begged my mom to please buy me at least one sheep or even a cow or something. She simply said, "Of course I will, when we're done shopping." However, when we finished shopping, the animals were nowhere in sight.

Luckily for me, my grandmother was not as clever with her excuses as my mother, and much more easily persuaded. Each time I went shopping with her, she would kindly buy me a beautiful white chicken that I could bring to their home as my pet. The problem was that these chickens refused to be domesticated and didn't like to be handled. It deeply hurt my feelings. I loved these animals with all my heart, and they wouldn't reciprocate. It wouldn't have mattered, though—I could barely get acquainted with my little chickies before the neighbor's fat white cat came slinking over the roof. When I wasn't around to protect my pet, the cat would jump into our yard to slaughter it. Fortunately, grandma always came through with another one the next day. It was no wonder that cat was so fat.

My relationship with my grandmother was typical: She spoiled me and never got upset at anything I did. She let me wear her most expensive high-heeled shoes and head scarves, even though she had to take a small hammer to her shoes afterward because I caused the heels to fall out of alignment as I dashed for the yard.

My grandfather was of Popolzai lineage, born in Kandahar, the same city where President Hamid Karzai's family was from. In fact, Karzai's parents' wedding took place at my grandparents' home. My grandfather was as loving with me as my grandmother was, though he did not extend that same courtesy to the rest of his grandchildren. To everyone else, he was strict and hot-tempered. Nobody had the nerve to approach him; they spoke to him only when spoken to. I soon discovered that I was an exception. Just to prove that he wouldn't get angry with me, I would purposely bump him from behind as he, dressed in a suit, drank his evening tea while listening to the radio. Though the hot tea burned him, he never said a word. If he restrained himself because he thought it would be the last time he ever saw me and wanted to make the visit as pleasant as possible, he was right. Indeed, I never saw him again after we left Afghanistan, and his kindness has been burned into my memory.

～❧ ❧～

Our smug taxi driver didn't get our spirits down. Our day on the town had been lots of fun. We were one week into our trip, and we were over our jet lag and settling in wonderfully.

Abruptly, the car came to a halt. We found ourselves in a strange and disturbing traffic jam. Our driver began to scream and honk at other cars, which honked and screamed back. I peeked out the window. Cars faced every direction. Then I noticed the tank pointing directly at our taxi. It was colossal. I looked away and sank into my seat, hoping that it would disappear.

Frantic, my mom tried to convince our driver to pull out of the jam and get out of there. He argued profusely with the other drivers who blocked his route. Everyone outside our cab was inflamed, angry, and frustrated. Inside, we were just frightened to death. My mom's two girlfriends were terrified. They began to pray to God, pleading for His mercy and for our safe return home. Their prayers worked. Somehow we managed to escape the jam and take side streets to get back to my grandparents' home.

When we were safely inside, we heard the news on the radio.

The national anthem was playing as the announcer loudly declared that Daoud Khan, the president of Afghanistan, had been assassinated. He had died at the hands of Afghans who toppled his regime to install a Communist government. The announcer said that his death was his own fault, caused by his refusal to surrender. The new president was Noor Mohammad Taraki, an Afghan Communist. The announcer said that anyone who opposed the new regime would be destroyed.

So once again, Afghanistan was presented with a president instead of a king. A kingship would have been distasteful to the

Communists; a president sounded truer to the ideals of equality. But such presidents were neither elected nor representative of Afghans. They terrorized people into obeying their rules and following their agendas. All government employees must comply with the new rules or be executed. And all passports would be frozen. This meant that nobody could enter or leave the country, indefinitely.

⚘ ⚘

My mother tried to protect me from the nightmare of the days that followed the coup. We could see planes flying overhead in the direction of the presidential palace, followed by terrible loud noises. The nights were even scarier, as the sounds of attacks and the showering of bombs shook the entire house. When I would suddenly wake up to ask her what was happening, she would smile and tell me not to worry: They were celebrating with fireworks, just as we would celebrate the Fourth of July in America. This made me happy, and I thought to myself that despite my expectations, Afghanistan had ended up being a really fun place.

Luckily, residential areas were not targets of the attacks. Bombings were focused on the presidential palace and on certain military bases that were resisting the takeover. But in all wars, intended targets are often missed and many civilian lives go unaccounted for. We were fortunate enough not to lose any family members. Still, the effects of the violence permeated all levels of society. There was a constant sense of fear. All the local shops shut down. A curfew was imposed, so everyone had to be in their homes before nightfall. Tanks and guards surrounded all the government agencies. Highly placed government officials, generals, high-ranking police officers, and members of the secret police who weren't Communists were arrested. Nobody knew what the new regime would bring. For now, all that could be seen, heard, or experienced was war and destruction.

It didn't feel like vacation anymore. We stopped going to get-togethers, shopping, sightseeing, and all of the other things we had done the first week. I became frustrated with my mom's excuses, and soon I realized that she wasn't telling me everything. This made me miss my dad even more, and I wanted to go home. As the weeks passed, the feeling of martial law subsided somewhat. Stores reopened, people ventured out in the daytime, and we resumed some of our trips. But the soldiers and tanks remained, and a general mood of uneasiness set in.

Our days in Afghanistan took on a routine. Most mornings, my mother left me with my grandparents while she went to government agencies to try to find a way home. The few times I went with her, I saw how the employees looked at her with wonder, asking her why she had picked such an awful time to come here. Her day's efforts yielded little, and she would start the process all over again the next morning.

My mother felt particularly pressured to get out in a hurry because my father, Qadeer, was not willing to wait and see what would happen next. After hearing the unbelievable news and finding that we were stuck in Afghanistan indefinitely, he began preparing to come to Kabul so we could at least be together. But my mother knew that if he did, he could be conscripted into the military, sent to fight against the loyalist resistance, and never seen again. Worse, he could be imprisoned as a spy for the United States. My father was still an Afghan citizen, but his coming from the U.S. would raise suspicion, since the new Taraki government was closely allied with the Soviet Union. The government would question why he had come at such an inopportune time. My parents battled it out on the phone for a long time, but my mom was firm that he stay put.

We later heard the story of one young man who, after coming to Afghanistan from the U.S., was arrested soon after his arrival and was persuaded to sign a plea bargain for his release. The deal was that he had to go on national television and admit to being a spy for the United States. The purpose, his captors told him, was to help warn Afghans of the possibility of American spies. After he "confessed," they would set him free. If he refused to comply, he would certainly be executed. Of course he agreed to their maniacal deal. But after confessing to all of the charges they brought against him, his televised interview was used as evidence to incriminate him, and he was sent to jail. For ten years this young man, who had graduated from college in the United States, suffered the tortures of living in an Afghan prison. But he was considered fortunate because he escaped with his life. When he was released and finally returned to America, he tried to pretend — perhaps devoutly wished — that all of that misery had never actually happened.

Afghanistan's system of conscription was to literally pick up men and boys from schools and colleges and pull them off the streets to join the military. No father, husband, or son was safe from forced conscription — unless, of course, he had connections in the government or knew someone with authority. Most citizens faced the horror of giving themselves and members of their family up to this most unwelcome war.

Many people talked about smuggling their sons out of the country to neighboring Pakistan or Iran. Others went to India. These countries served the purpose that Canada has played in the past for Americans who wished to escape the draft. The difference, though, is that Americans could travel to Canada fairly comfortably, whereas Afghans had to hire smugglers at hefty prices to help them walk through the mountains to the neighboring countries. Further, these smugglers were generally shady characters, criminals. Some people paid smugglers their entire life savings only to be abandoned in the middle of the trip in Afghanistan's mountains, where government helicopters frequently patrolled and bombed anything that moved. Other smugglers simply killed their clients and fled with their money. Despite all this, a person's chances with smugglers seemed more favorable than those of a soldier. So my mother worked desperately to get us out of the country as quickly as possible, before my father showed up in Kabul.

≈ ≈

In the midst of all this turmoil, our family decided to take a break and vacation in the city of Paghman. The family often spent the warmer months there to escape Kabul's hot summers. Paghman proved to be a true oasis from the chaos we had been experiencing. We stayed at my aunt's beautiful two-story house, where a stream flowed through the backyard. The sky there was a gorgeous blue. Lush cherry trees gave a sweet smell to the air, which was crisp and refreshingly clean.

Children and teenagers came to the house to take my aunt's orders for Afghan delicacies such as fresh-baked bread, homemade butter, *bolani* (pastries filled with green vegetables), and *qaymagh* (cream shavings made by boiling whole milk and slowly stripping the skin off the top many times). They would prepare and deliver the dishes the same day, so everything was fresh. We had these foods for breakfast along with sweet tea. We usually spent lunch at the outdoor kabob houses where we ate *kabob sikhi*, lamb kabob, while surrounded by flowers and greenery. Each order of kabob sikhi included ten skewers of very tender meat for the low price of ten Afghanis. Some of my relatives enjoyed *chaynaki*, a delicacy made by placing meat and vegetables inside a tea kettle and baking it well in a tandoor oven. After eating such fattening food, we washed it down with some of Paghman's water, reputed to be among the best in the world. It was said that if you ate a rock, the water from Paghman had the power to digest it for you.

Despite their healthy appetites, people in Paghman were slim and trim. Part of this was because they walked a lot. That was no wonder, as the city was a Garden of Eden, a feast for all the senses. I had a wonderful time playing there with my cousins, running through the yard between the cherry trees. This is the beautiful country I have fond memories of, memories that now seem like a faint dream.

We were unable to visit Jalalabad, home of the famous *Bagh Shahi*, or royal garden. My grandparents had a vacation house there where they usually spent the colder months, as Kabul's winters were harsh. Jalalabad was east of Kabul, not too far from Pakistan. Well known for its orange groves and *chapli kabob* (beef kabob), it was a safe place where women and children could freely roam well into the evening hours without fearing for their safety. This is the same Jalalabad that was laid waste by bombings beginning with the Soviet war and continuing through the "war on terrorism," which made dead bodies and rubble the city's main attractions. It is sad that modern images of Afghanistan are always of disaster and ruin, leading people to believe that it never contained a civilization.

My grandfather was anxious for us to visit his winter home, but my mom decided to take us instead to Mazar-e Sharif, home of the grand blue-tiled mosque in which the caliph Ali, son-in-law of the Prophet Muhammad (pbuh), is believed to be entombed. It was a gorgeous monument inside and out, made all the more poignant by the white doves that flocked to it. There we saw visitors tying beautiful fabrics to posts that had been placed there for that purpose. The knots that they tied symbolized a problem that needed passage and resolution. Once their prayers were accepted, they untied the fabric and gave charity as a display of gratitude.

After three long months, about two weeks before our originally planned date of return to America, the ministry of foreign affairs finally granted us permission to leave Afghanistan. First, though, my mother had to obtain a citizenship card that validated that she was in fact an Afghan *(shunakht-pass)*. Getting this validation was an even harder feat than getting permission to leave, because obviously she was married, but she couldn't legally leave the country without her husband's permission. Since her husband was in America, she would have to get permission from her husband's brother, who lived in the student dormitories of the Farrah province hundreds of miles away. The great distance and circumstances made it impossible for my uncle to travel to Kabul to give the required permission.

Every day that went by we were on shakier ground. Finally, my mom took a chance and decided to change her marital status to single. She filled out some new documentation that indicated she was single so that there would be no procedural requirement for her husband's permission. Of course, this left me as the problem child.

Unbelievably, all went well. Nobody questioned the fact that she had once applied as a married woman. My presence surely complicated the situation, but it seemed that the clerks wanted to help us out, believing our circumstances to be exceptional. My final image was of my teary-eyed grandfather waving good-bye at the airport as our plane pulled away, headed back to California. Home seemed like a completely different world. The place I had left behind seemed like a dream in another person's life. It was hard to accept that it was real.

⤚ ⤙

Before I left for Afghanistan in 1978, people didn't know where or what Afghanistan was. When someone asked me where I was from — a question often provoked by my Eastern features — my reply usually caused a look of puzzlement, and my questioner then asked if it was located anywhere near Egypt or perhaps Africa. At a tender age I became tired of such questions and wished I didn't have to explain who I was.

After we returned, many Americans suddenly did know where Afghanistan was. The events were significant to Americans in light of the Cold War, since the new Afghan government was allied with the hated Red Army. However, instead of pictures of high mountains cradling fertile valleys and clear blue skies, now the only images of Afghanistan that people saw were of war, blood-

shed, starvation, and all the things that demean the very foundation of our existence.

We had been in Afghanistan during its final days of happiness,
peace, and freedom. We were home now, but we left a country full
of innocent and good people, with all their hopes and aspirations,
behind in the dust.

⚜ *Two* ⚜

Afghans in America

Before events took a turn for the worse in Afghanistan, my small family had lived a relatively quiet life, and my parents' friends formed the core of our social circle. But as our extended family and the families of my parents' friends flocked to safety in America, a new dynamic took over and ended our carefree days. We became consumed with shuffling relatives to government offices to get their documentation straight, driving them to doctors' appointments, helping them find housing, and enrolling their children in school. They relied on us to help them build a new foundation for their lives in a foreign country. By the end of the decade, virtually everyone in both my parents' families was situated in the United States. The last to come was an aunt who stayed in Afghanistan to bail her son out of prison; he had been falsely accused of treason by the Communist regime. She came to America with him in 1993.

My mom's parents, the ones who had flown to Los Angeles for her wedding so many years ago, did not emigrate. My grandfather insisted that he must stay in his homeland, and my grandmother was not willing to leave him behind. One day my mother received a letter from the aunt who was in Kabul with her imprisoned son. The letter said that my grandmother was ill. Immediately, my mother tried to call her, but because of the war, you had to make an appointment a week in advance to place a phone call. My mother wanted to get through immediately. After pleading with one supervisor after another until two o'clock in the morning, she gave up and made her appointment to place a call to her mother the following week.

A couple of days later, a cousin called and asked to speak to my mother. When we gave the phone to her, my mother began crying profusely. When my father asked her what had happened, she just kept saying "My mother, my mother."

Our entire family got together and listened to tapes of the Quran. The women covered their hair in *gach* Afghan scarves. We held an event called the *fatiha* at the mosque in my grandmother's memory, as is customary for Afghans. Afterward everyone who attended came to our house, where food was served and grieving family members were comforted and attended to.

For months to follow, my mom dressed in dark colors. Every so often I saw her staring blankly, as if in a trance. I noticed that when I came home from school, the living room was filled with smoke. I supposed she had taken up smoking to calm her nerves.

About a year and a half later, another dreadful call came from my mother's brother, who lived in Los Angeles. He didn't tell her why, but urged her to come to his house right away. We got in the car and my mother drove extremely fast, though she wasn't normally in the habit of speeding. For some reason the normally crowded 405 freeway felt abandoned, as though we were the only ones on the road. When we got to my uncle's house and he opened the door, I heard him as well as everyone else inside wailing. My grandfather had died.

The deaths of my grandparents scarred my mother and her siblings emotionally. They carry the guilt of not being able to be with their parents in their last days, of not burying them or attending their funeral processions. Only two of my mother's sisters were there to take care of their parents when they fell ill and died. Though the Soviet invasion did not cost my family their lives, it paralyzed them emotionally for life. My mother would often tell me, "My parents had eight children. What good were we when they died alone and had to be buried by strangers?"

~❧ ❧~

My parents worked very hard to build lives in America. My dad adopted a very strong work ethic that bordered on workaholism. While it helped our family's upward mobility, the zeal with which he applied himself to his job created many conflicts. It was this work ethic that prevented him from accompanying my mother and me on our trip to Afghanistan in 1978. People were not under so much pressure in Afghanistan to work as hard as he did; there is no word for "stress" in the Dari vocabulary. But my dad was sucked into the modern capitalist work culture that demands all your resources if you want to stay competitive. He said that he would either do the job right or not at all, but nothing in between.

My father was not the only one who adopted such a stringent work ethic. Many Afghan men felt the traditional calling to be their families' breadwinners and were prepared to do so at all costs. Indeed, women and children also were plunged into the work culture, as their participation was usually necessary to sustain their livelihood. Of course, immigrants who had been uneducated or had no financial means in Afghanistan viewed the opportunity to work and live independently in the U.S. as a huge breakthrough, a giant leap in their family's economic potential. But most people who had the means to come to the U.S. had been educated and were in relatively good positions in Afghanistan. Now they were forced either to take jobs unrelated to their fields of expertise or to do substandard work that didn't employ their true talents, as these were the only jobs available for people who didn't speak English properly. Whether they fell into better positions or worse, they formed a class of people who worked zealously to support their families, and they led frugal lives while enduring a great deal of what most people would call humiliation.

Humiliation was endured primarily by Afghans who could not communicate well in English. They were made fun of because of their accents and the way they spoke. They were spoken to in loud voices as if to penetrate some kind of sound barrier. They were talked down to and treated as inferior. Unable to communicate complex thoughts in their limited English vocabulary, they were treated as though they were unable to have complex thoughts at all. These Afghans felt belittled, and the feeling added a great deal of this new thing called "stress" to their lives.

One such person who went through this was a family friend who had been a military general in Afghanistan. Since he didn't have a U.S. driver's license, on one occasion I decided to drive him around to help him do his day's business. I was astonished at how his strong, commanding military personality was transformed in a matter of minutes. When the checkout girl at the grocery store asked him if he wanted paper or plastic, he was confused, so he smiled goofily and said "What?" She immediately grew impatient and retorted in a voice that was loud and excruciatingly slow, "Do you want me to put your groceries in paper bags or plastic bags?" He apologized profusely, saying, "Paper bags, please, thank you very much." She didn't reply or say "You're welcome." Instead, she rolled her eyes and greeted the next customer.

Those who were on public assistance also tell of the shameful manner in which they were treated in social service offices, the long lines they were expected to wait in, and how they were treated and spoken to by people who were often much younger than they were. One of my Afghan acquaintances from school said that she had to go everywhere with her family to translate for them, but that she hated going to the dreaded grocery store because of the condescending looks she received when her parents pulled out their food stamps at the checkout stand.

It was a race for survival, and Afghans found themselves working extremely hard to achieve the American dream: a home, a car, and the simple need for peace. Unfortunately, it proved to be a myth for those who could barely keep their heads above water. Career advancement was a distant goal, and became something that parents eventually wished for their children rather than for themselves.

Wherever I looked, whether at the mosque, school, or grocery store, I found other Eastern cultures thriving and progressing so *normally*. These Arabs, Iranians, Armenians, Indians, and others of Eastern descent seemed to be in a better social position than the Afghans I knew. In fact, whenever I noticed Afghans, I noticed their failures. These failures ranged from socioeconomic position to spirituality. Presumably I belonged to their "community," yet I couldn't relate to them. I couldn't understand why I was so different from other Afghans in my community and in my own age group, and why their parents were so different from my own.

It didn't occur to me until later how different my parents' situation had been from most Afghan immigrants. When my parents came to the U.S. in their early twenties, they were both educated. At first they held menial jobs at local restaurants or university cafeterias; they lived in dorms and walked to and from work without a vehicle. But in due time they managed to own property, raise children, and move on with life like everyone else in American society. They came here of their own free will during a peaceful time in Afghanistan, years before the Soviet invasion. They were as prepared as they could be to start a new life in a foreign land. They seemed so in control of their livelihood, so able to communicate effectively with others on all levels of society. They seemed so much more open-minded to me than the closed-off immigrants I knew who came after them.

On the other hand, Afghans who came to America during the Soviet invasion were refugees seeking asylum. They had been forced out of their homeland. They had never planned to leave the homes, businesses, and families that they had spent their lifetimes building. They fled through the mountains with nothing more than the clothing on their backs. They came here with no money to speak of and without the skills or English necessary to get along in the American workforce. Many had to take advantage of public housing. It was sad to see these former ministers and high-ranking officials of a proud country brought to such a demeaning level. For them, coming to America was not an improvement on their previous lifestyles but a step down. My family knew such officials, who were now working several menial jobs just to meet basic needs.

One acquaintance, Zaman, had held a high position in a foreign ministry in Afghanistan. He was pampered by the government, and he and his family were given many privileges and luxuries. Eventually he became an Afghan official in Bombay, where he moved in diplomatic circles that sometimes included popular Indian actors such as Amitabh Bachan. He was respected, revered, and received graciously at extravagant social occasions and lavish dinner parties attended by government officials from various countries. Zaman says, "Afghanistan was really Afghanistan back then. I was highly honored for coming from such a strong nation of people." Most Afghan refugees are now disturbed at the depiction of their country as ruined and backward, because they fear people might think this is the way Afghanistan always was. Zaman tried to convince me that Afghanistan was a real nation when he was growing up, a progressive nation which he felt absolutely honored and privileged to be a part of.

When the nation was turned upside down by the Russians, Zaman came to the United States. As a result of his ability to read, write, and speak English, he was able to take some tests to become a public bus driver. Indeed, he was one of the most successful of his peers, who had become janitors, security guards, cab drivers, and laborers. He felt he had at least done well for himself compared to his colleagues.

Zaman tells me that while he was driving people from place to place, some passengers would look down upon him, insult the country he was from, and make him feel very small. In one instance, when he was driving for a group tour, one of the passengers asked him where he was from. Zaman replied "Afghanistan," and the passenger promptly began to bash the country, its value systems, practices, and politics. When the bus finally arrived at its destination, Zaman told the gentleman that he wouldn't charge him for the ride. When the passenger asked why, he replied, "You talk like Afghan people are trash, but we are not trash. I am not interested in your money. You keep your money. I refuse to accept it from you." Zaman says that refusing to take the man's money was the only part of the situation that he could control. He wanted to show this person that Afghan people are very proud and honorable despite what the man thought of them.

The difference between earlier and later immigrants caused something of a split in the Afghan community. The earlier immigrants were more advanced socially, academically, and financially, and were usually better socialized than the later immigrants. Some of the later immigrants' children felt the need to become involved in white-collar crime, such as credit card fraud, to "catch up" with and perhaps beat the other immigrants economically. Many younger Afghan immigrants of this group could not focus on their educations, since they were too busy trying to feed themselves and maintain a minimum standard of life. Yet others who did not wish to accept this endless struggle found a cynical solution in youth gangs. Afghan youth gangs were particularly abhorred by immigrants who had fled Afghanistan due to violence; at least there was an honorable cause in Afghanistan, but in America there was no justification for this brand of violence.

Another interesting split occurred in the global Afghan community, between those who settled in Europe and those who went to the United States. Afghans in Europe are seen as being more conservative and diligent about preserving their Afghan identity than their American compatriots. These Afghan-Europeans are said to look down upon Afghan-Americans because they view us as generally more liberal and distant from true Afghan ideals and culture. Among a people who have been displaced from their homeland on such a grand scale, losing that identity is considered dangerous.

Indeed, mass migration to foreign lands created a new dynamic in the Afghan psyche. Preservation of Afghan language, cultural values, and moral and religious identity became a great priority, as they were largely incompatible with Western norms and thus very vulnerable. Afghans couldn't take their heritage and language for granted, as they would surely be lost over time if not attended to.

Throughout my childhood, my father struggled to make Farsi the primary language in our home. Any time a shred of English slipped from my lips, my dad quickly yelled "FARSI!"—even if he was on the other side of the house. One evening, I was chatting with my mom as my dad dozed on the couch. We were speaking in a mishmash of English and Farsi. My dad, in his sleep, told me to speak in Farsi. My mom began laughing hysterically at the baffled expression on my face. He knew what language I was speaking even while unconscious! He strictly enforced the "no English at home" rule until my early college years, when he finally threw in the towel. Now he speaks with us mostly in English.

My dad always played Afghan music at home and even in the car. He would translate it for me, even though I couldn't have cared less what was being said, and I implored him to play the radio instead. It wasn't until years later that the music on those old eight-tracks and cassettes became the music I love most. There is such depth in the poetry that it is like being swept into a sea of emotions. I find myself translating those same songs to my younger brother and sister when we are at Afghan concerts, or in the car when they would prefer to listen to the radio. But at the time, as my father struggled to preserve his cultural values in our family, I struggled to lead a socially normal life in American society.

I was the focus of much of my father's child-rearing energy throughout the twenty-two years that I lived at home. Because I was the first child, my dad had the most energy and patience in the prime of his youth to discipline me. My younger brother and sister, on the other hand, get away with murder. I suppose I must have worn him out. But it also seems that when I was growing up, the Afghan community in America was much more traditional than it was when my siblings were teenagers. Afghan adults seem to have progressively compromised and become more lenient in applying their rigid cultural rules to the youth. Such leniency was probably more necessary in families with many children; how else could an exhausted parent maintain household peace, sanity, and unity?

How Afghans carried on their traditions in America often reflected how they had lived in Afghanistan. My family lived by the norms of its particular social set: Pashtuns who had lived in Kabul for generations, spoke only Dari, and were more Westernized and urbanized, in contrast to Afghans who had lived in the country's rural areas their entire lives. My family is intermixed with many ethnic groups, thus expanding the breadth of my experience with an ethnically diverse people. My parents' more modern mentality did not mean that they were disconnected from their heritage. It just meant that they viewed education as a priority. They, like their own parents, were not intimidated into keeping their daughters from going to school based on old standards of acceptability. The women in our family were given more rights and a greater say in how they dressed, whom they decided to marry, and how they conducted their lives. In sum, my parents were less other-directed, yet still maintained high expectations. They were more concerned with the happiness and well-being of their family than with what others thought of them, but within the parameters of Afghan social norms. They felt that deviating from these norms would foster sadness and turmoil.

Even with compromise, many Afghan parents I knew growing up feared American music, dress, slang, and the more extreme hairstyles. All these things were viewed as inherently bad. If Afghan boys or girls listened to heavy metal or other hard brands of American music and had the hairdos to go with it, they were viewed as problem children, rebellious and untraditional teenagers who would undoubtedly damage their own reputations and their families'.

My father exhibited these fears about living in such an open society. During my early teens, he got the idea in his head that I was a punk rocker and scrutinized every stitch of clothing I bought. I'm still puzzled as to where he picked up the "punk" notion and how he defined it in his mind. I'm certain it had something to do with my fascination with Madonna, but I did not relate to punk rockers in any way. He expected me to dress in a very basic conservative fashion, wearing dark, formal colors and clothing that was very boyish with no style whatsoever. He believed that school was a serious institution and a place only for education, and that students should not be dressing up to go there but simply to study and return straight home. In effect, he wanted me to look like what I thought of as the out-of-place FOBs—"fresh off the boat" immigrants who had been raised in Afghanistan.

I slowly began to realize that he wanted to conceal my looks to divert attention from me. As long as I didn't stand out, no one would ever get up the nerve to show a love interest in me or eventually propose marriage. Therefore, if I wore something that complemented my figure or complexion, he definitely did not like it. But if the clothing made me look like a boy, he loved it and thought it was perfect regardless of the price.

My struggle with my father seemed to me to be more intense because I was a girl. For Afghans, girls are seen as more vulnerable than boys. While a girl's reputation is paramount to both her own social success and her family's, a boy her age is not held to such harsh standards and is free to do as he pleases, with no accountability or real social consequences. While a girl[1] absolutely

---

[1] I use the term "girl" as it is used in Dari, to distinguish between wed and unwed females; a girl is an unmarried virgin, and a woman is married.

must be a virgin at marriage, a boy is not expected to be. A girl should not have had prior relationships; this is not even a question with a boy. Thus Afghan boys and men in America seem to have had a much easier time assimilating, as there are no severe social constraints upon them. These young men were free to indulge in all that the new society offered them, with no fear of social persecution or taboos.

All social activities outside of school were banned for me and for the other Afghan girls I knew, as were all clothes that were not uniformly conservative. But following these mandates did not always protect me from criticism. As I got older, I was usually blamed if a suitor approached the family. I grew to hate suitors because of the hostility they created at home. On one occasion, my dad actually hit a guy who wanted me to marry his brother. They came from a family that my dad considered to be of low class — not with regard to their ethnicity or financial position, but to their strength of character and principles. A person's *substance* was always considered key.

My parents believe that class is more important than wealth, education, or anything else that a person can acquire, since class cannot be achieved or attained. They define class as the values, mores, principles, and mannerisms that one has learned from birth through one's family. They are all part of the principle of *ghaiyrat*, Afghan pride. This is an honor code that affects every facet of an Afghan's life and is viewed as imperative to character. As far as my parents are concerned, one can spend a few years to become educated and work hard to acquire wealth, cars, expensive clothes, and so forth, but class is entrenched in the fabric of an individual's substance. In the case of the unfortunate suitor's brother, my dad was insulted that he even asked for my hand in marriage.

My dad had a hot temper. He never laid a hand on me, but with a look he could make me weep, and he could say things to pierce my heart. Similarly, with a different look, he communicated volumes about how much he loved and cared for me. He has never told me that he loves me, nor has he ever needed to, as his actions quite clearly tell me that he does. I have never told him that I love him, but I always respect and obey his wishes and show him how highly I regard him and my mother without the need for words. My efforts to become their ideal daughter was how I showed them that I loved them—with actions rather than words, which are as fleeting as the wind. Growing up I thought I had the strictest, roughest dad in the world, whose sole goal was to make my life miserable. But in hindsight, I think the combination of my mom's and dad's parental styles and philosophies worked out to yield a unique bunch who managed to make it through life just fine, if not easily.

Other girls were not so fortunate, as their families put excessive pressure on them and emphasized matters that seemed trivial to me. I knew many girls who were expected to cook and clean up after their brothers and father after coming home from school, and who were beaten by all male members of their family if they did not cooperate or showed any sign of rebellion. Their homework or other school-related obligations were not treated with great importance; their main purpose was to serve their families. These girls did not have to go to school or become great successes because they were expected to marry and have husbands to support them.

A girl I knew by the name of Palwasha lived such a life. We went to the same school. We had our heritage in common, and I thought we would have much more in common as well. We first met in the girl's gym locker room, hastily changing clothes to run out to the field for our physical education class. She asked me where I was from, and I knew immediately that she, like everyone else who asked me where I was from, meant my national heritage. I assumed that she was Iranian, because I had never met an Afghan girl in school before. When I said "Afghanistan," her eyes lit up and she said, "Oh my God, me too!"

We were both very pleased to have met, and we struck up a friendship that unfortunately didn't last. As our friendship evolved, I discovered more about the dark side of her life. She wore sunglasses from time to time to cover her black eyes, and some mornings it just seemed that her mind was somewhere else. She eventually opened up to me and told me about her father, whom she said she hated to death. She said, "He always picks on me because he thinks I'm too quick to stand up to him. I do all of the housework. I serve him and my two brothers their dinner, which I cook when I get home from school. I clean the house and iron their clothes and at the end of the night when I try to do some homework, he will find an excuse to pick on me and hit me for doing something wrong. And all I do is take care of him!" She said that if she even talked to her brothers in too loose a manner, she would be scorned by her father. She attempted suicide on many occasions by taking pills from the medicine cabinet and visited the hospital often for related problems.

After high school, her family moved to a new home farther away. But Palwasha refused to live there, and simply ran away. It was a risky decision. She was an adult and over eighteen years old, but traditional Afghan girls don't leave home until they are married. Leaving would isolate her from the community. By walking out on her family, she would lose her reputation, which would eliminate her prospects of marriage in the Afghan community — and she had no higher education or means of supporting herself. Furthermore, it would look like the situation was her fault rather than her father's. I thought that she might be able to reconcile her situation by appealing to other members of her family, such as her uncle, who could intervene with her father. But our relationship dwindled as her rage toward her father grew. In the end, she felt that I was on her family's side and that I didn't understand her anymore. Palwasha married an American man and moved on with her life.

My father made it unequivocally clear to me and my siblings

that all of his children would marry only within the Afghan heritage. His only open-mindedness on this subject was his lack of bias toward marrying us only to people from our own Mohammadzai lineage. Any upstanding Afghan would do. My dad defined an upstanding Afghan as someone who had all of the mannerisms and characteristics of a true Afghan. Educational or material wealth was not the primary concern. In this sense, there was no evidence of ethnic bias among the various Afghan ethnic groups in our family. Though my father is Pashtun by heritage, he would not require us to marry only Pashtuns.

Intermarriage between Pashtuns and Farsi-speakers, or Tajiks, is not uncommon. In most Afghan families, one does not find pure homogeneity of ethnic background. As in other societies, people tended to pair up with those whom they were attracted to, shared common beliefs with, and so forth. Ethnic diversity in Afghanistan was more celebrated than hated before the deep divisions that transpired following the Soviet invasion. Afghanistan was not a melting pot but a salad bowl of cultures that shared a common nationality, just as we see in the United States. However, even in the U.S., different cultures have taken on varying roles, depending on historical context. Even though it is a stable society, the U.S. continues to struggle in moving from a white Anglo-Saxon Protestant mentality toward accepting people from *all* races who call themselves American. The same struggle exists in Afghanistan.

My father used to tell me stories of Afghans who had emigrated for Australia generations ago during the British invasion of Afghanistan and who had since become mixed with many other races. He had met one gentleman who looked and spoke as if he were an indigenous Australian, but who told him that his ancestors were actually from Afghanistan. My dad told me that this was heart-wrenching for him, because it was a sad and indirect consequence of the foreign invasions of Afghanistan. To him it was clear that the preservation of the Afghan race depended on a commitment to marry only among Afghans.

I used to question my dad a great deal, especially when I was in high school, as to why he imposed such nationalistic values upon his children when nationalism contradicted Islamic principles. I pointed out that under Islam, people should choose their marriage partners first by their religion, which transcends ethnic and racial boundaries. This would mean that any good, upstanding Muslim should be fairly considered as a prospect.

My father vehemently and adamantly disagreed with this. He believed and continues to believe that the fact that so many millions of Afghans have been displaced from their homeland and forced to assimilate in various cultures is an issue of grave concern for the future and preservation of the Afghan race. He believes that if Afghans begin to wed non-Afghans, mixing their bloodlines, watering down their traditions and values, and forgetting their language, then the Afghan race will be significantly damaged and eventually lost. He also notes that those Afghans who now reside in Western countries are among the best and brightest that the country had to offer, because they were the ones who had the wealth, education, and opportunity to leave. If this cream of the crop were to dilute itself more than it already has, then the future of the country would be terribly grim, he thought.

Most other Afghan parents that I've known prefer that their children marry Afghans, especially when those parents are older Afghans who speak only Dari. They wish to be able to communicate with new members of the family. They want them to be able to understand the delicate matters of cultural norms and etiquette that are ever so subtle and difficult to teach to an outsider. Yet a fair number of Afghan youth continue to marry outside the Afghan circle, either to Westerners or to those from other parts of the Middle East. In these cases, some Afghan families request that the new family member convert to the religion of Islam, especially when their daughter is marrying someone of a different faith.

Intercultural marriages are generally acceptable only for men and far less accepted for Afghan girls. There is an odd Afghan

mentality that considers the offspring of sons to relate more closely
to the family than those of daughters. Before my grandmother
passed away, she told us how she wanted her jewelry divided.
With the exception of a few small pieces, she gave all of it to her
sons' boys to give to their future wives. Her only daughter received none, nor did any of her sons' daughters. I thought that
these outsiders would never cherish or truly appreciate the senti-
mental value of her jewelry. But she explained to me that when a
girl gets married, her children are considered to be more a part of
her husband's family than her own. Upon marriage, the girl is seen
as parted from her family and bonded with her new groom's family. Boys bring their brides into their own families, and his children take his family's last name.

I felt that this was a bit backward, since in my own experience
Afghan girls make an extra effort to stay close to their families,
and I do not see the same level of effort on the part of the boys in
the community. In any event, daughters are simply not as highly
regarded as sons in a cultural context, perhaps as a result of the
impact they can have on their families' reputations. A girl can
quite easily break her father's name in the community with a bad
move or by unwittingly making a natural mistake, so common in
life for young people. I think that making one's own mistakes can
prove more valuable than never taking the chances and risks that
allow learning and growth. But such mistakes sometimes prove ir-
reversible in the Afghan community, and the consequences can
leave a family socially shattered. There is no room for later correc-
tion of a serious human error. Once stained, a girl's reputation is
difficult to reconstitute in Afghan society. While more broad-
minded Afghans do not share in this traditional view and I have
not seen it outwardly expressed by my parents, I definitely feel
that they are more at ease with their sons because of the lack of
worry involved and their inability to create as much heartache on
a social level.

My sister and brother are both in their early twenties and will soon have to deal with the nationalistic rules of marriage that my dad has implemented in our family. It is interesting to see them go through the same process I did, particularly inasmuch as they disagree with the cultural restriction on marriage. They too like to point out that Islam permits Muslims from all ethnic backgrounds to marry one another. Others in their age group struggle to find mates who are Afghan so that they can please their families. The whole process of marriage still seems awkward in terms of where young Afghans can meet, how courtship takes place, and the subsequent wedding and living arrangements.

Interestingly enough, all of the youth that I have encountered insist that they would love to marry an Afghan, as long as he or she is the right one. But finding the right Afghan to marry continues to be a struggle, since Afghans have become scattered, and young people are not organized into networks that will allow them opportunities to become acquainted with one another. Most who marry non-Afghans do so because they were unsuccessful in finding an Afghan that they were compatible with. But there are plenty of fine young Afghan men and women out there—we just have to find the means to reconnect in our new environments.

Another problem with finding the right match within the community comes from trying to follow parental standards of what a "proper spouse" should be within the contemporary realities of the Afghan-American community. In other words, despite their own actions, Afghan boys, who are the pursuers of marriage, are taught to look for a pure Afghan girl who is innocent, respectful, from a good family, and beautiful. The term "innocent" is loaded, since it carries the expectation that a girl not drink, smoke, go to night clubs, have premarital sex, dress provocatively, travel, go to school away from her parents—the list goes on and on. By and large, first-generation Afghan-American girls in California have departed from this norm (with the exception of being beautiful), some more than others. Thus, the boys who may or may not be upstanding or impressive themselves find it difficult to find a suitable match based on their parents' expectations.

Afghan-American girls have gained more financial independence and have excelled academically. They are not as desperate for a husband who will take care of them. This dynamic has been blamed for the relatively high divorce rate among Afghans living abroad, since women no longer depend on their husbands and therefore don't need to stay married. The taboo against marrying divorcées has also softened up a bit among more liberal Afghans, which means that a divorced woman's fate is not necessarily sealed. To further complicate matters, many girls who resent the double standard take action against it. Boys are permitted to indulge in all of society's pleasures, whereas girls are expected to stay sheltered at home. But many Afghan girls defy these standards and refuse to marry a person who has been shamelessly promiscuous while expecting to settle down with a "pure" Muslim Afghan girl; they simply find it unfair.

Afghan boys who are influenced by the notion that they must find an innocent Afghan girl would prefer to marry an American who is not a virgin than an Afghan girl who is not a virgin, since it is taboo for an Afghan girl but not necessarily for an American. If an American girl is promiscuous, it is excused on the grounds of the social norms under which she has been raised.

However, Afghan boys who live abroad do not always uphold the traditional morals that men do in Afghanistan. Afghan men who live in Afghanistan are not socially accepted if they behave in the manner of Afghan men who live abroad. Still, the effect of the Afghan double standard is that such boys do not have to suffer consequences for their negligence, while girls must pay a high price.

Certainly, a sizable portion of Afghan-Americans in their early twenties find themselves leading untraditional lives by the definition of an Afghan living in Afghanistan. Those who cling to their cultural traditions are a minority and a rare commodity in California, yet many mothers are busily searching for them to marry their unwed sons and daughters. In the West, where mainstream society runs by a totally different set of norms, not only is it difficult to find an "authentic" Afghan, it is difficult to *be* an "authentic" Afghan. Young people are put in the position of having to lead Afghan lifestyles under their parents' watch while leading Western lifestyles outside the home so that they can get along in mainstream society.

Expecting children to lead a wholly Afghan lifestyle at home while they are trying to lead a normal and socialized American lifestyle outside has led to identity crises, double-life syndromes, and various other personality complexes—even suicides. On a cable television program called "Teen Talk" where I used to appear, Afghan teens talked about these very problems. One Afghan girl said that in high school she would ask her teachers, "Did you know that I lead a double life?" Of course, they had no idea. She talked about how she could never confess her feelings for fear of reprisal. She felt that her parents never understood her or the society they were living in, and that they expected their children to continue living in every way as if they were still in Afghanistan.

～※ ※～

Surely, those Afghans who were able to escape to America were the lucky ones. Still, leaving one's homeland with no realistic chance of returning is traumatic. When you uproot a plant from its original habitat and replant it somewhere foreign, it is rare that no fracture occurs. Some die right away; others suffer slowly with illness; yet others persevere but remain sad and wilted their entire lives.

My Shair Kaka, my dad's vivacious youngest brother who had chased me in roller skates and bought me ice cream in Kabul, followed this pattern. He came to America well into the Soviet war. He had experienced terrible things; once he protected my young cousins during a Soviet shootout in the streets by throwing himself over their bodies. Yet he grew up to be a fun-loving, intelligent, and handsome man. He felt that leaving Afghanistan spelled the end of his happy days.

Only a few years after coming to the U.S., at the age of 34, Shair Kaka was diagnosed with cancer. After having survived the chaos of the Soviet invasion and all of the havoc that it wreaked in Afghanistan, he refused to succumb. In his last days, when the doctors wanted to stop all treatment to let him die as comfortably as possible, he refused to let them. He said that he would not die without a fight, and that is how he did it—in his own Afghan way. After a decade-long battle, he finally passed on in July 2002. He was a true uncle and a true friend.

The bulk of the Afghan population has been scattered about the globe, involuntarily uprooted from its original environment and planted in nations that do not resemble Afghanistan. These Afghans' identities have been challenged and fractured. They struggle violently to survive and preserve themselves in lands that they never would have known but for the historical accident that transformed the bright country of Afghanistan into a land of darkness.

~ Three ~

Coming Together, Falling Apart

Afghans who were fortunate enough to escape Afghanistan with their lives had to overcome tremendous social, economic, and spiritual struggles. Their perfectly good lives were entirely disrupted. They abandoned their homes and all their possessions, endured being thrust into the socialization process in foreign lands, and had to raise children who were less connected to or interested in their beliefs. And they were and continue to be angered by the direct cause of their disheveled lifestyles — the Russians.

The Russians really did a number on Afghanistan. They destroyed the very foundation and backbone of the country. They ruined Afghanistan so effectively that even more than a decade after they left, Afghans have been literally unable to get off the ground and stand on their own two feet. The cost to Afghanistan in human lives and infrastructure was so great that some kind of war reparations is in order and long overdue, even though the idea of trying to calculate such a number boggles the mind.

Of course, the Russians claimed to have had the best of intentions: They wanted to spread the Communist doctrine to the country to save it and help it progress. But the reality shows that they sinned terribly against humanity. The Communist doctrine was a myth that didn't save even its own people, let alone help the other countries it claimed to help. Its most effective use was to wreak havoc on people's lives in order to gain full control over them. It was not a merciful mission that the Soviets were looking to expand, but an empire. In 1979, sixty years after gaining independence from Great Britain, the people of Afghanistan found themselves again being used and attacked by foreign forces.

The Soviets became infamous for the crimes against humanity that they committed in Afghanistan. It wasn't enough that they invaded a sovereign nation; had its leaders assassinated; imprisoned and executed dissidents; imposed their ideology on a people who didn't welcome it; and bombed cities both ancient and modern to rubble. The atrocities they inflicted upon *noncombatants* are bloodcurdling. Russian soldiers tied Afghans down and ran them over with tanks or bulldozed them into mass graves. They raped young girls as well as pregnant women, who were then stabbed in the stomach with bayonets, to curtail the expansion of the Afghan race. These cowardly crimes of torture and murder were unjustified by war or any other standard that would attempt to assign meaning to such barbaric acts of terrorism.

During the Soviet occupation, Afghans lost close to one and a half million lives (the Soviets lost fifty thousand). Afghans continue to be killed or crippled by the barbaric land mines with which the Soviets riddled the country. Today, Afghanistan is the most heavily mined country in the world. Physicians Against Land Mines (PALM) reports that most of these mines were laid by the Soviets and pro-Soviet Afghan regimes between 1979 and 1992. According to PALM, before U.S. involvement in Afghanistan in 2001, these mines caused nearly ninety Afghan casualties per month. But during the American campaign against the Taliban in 2001, as refugees fled across heavily mined provinces to get to safety in Pakistan and Iran, this number may have grown even higher. During the campaign, an American soldier fell victim to a Soviet land mine; his leg had to be amputated as a result of the explosion.

Mines have left more than a million people in Afghanistan unable to work or lead normal lives. Worse, often the mines are disguised as beautiful toys, dolls, and other desirable-looking objects to fool children into drawing near. This cruel trick has led to the disfiguration of the future generation of Afghans. One girl's story, which I followed through the course of several years, is particularly harrowing to me. I will call the girl Hawa.

Hawa used to preface her story by saying that she was a young girl living in turbulent times in a country in which she had no source of play, amusement, or joy. She did not have what should be normal for every child: toys, amusement parks, playgrounds, a neighborhood safe from violence. One morning she was outside her home with some of the neighbor's children when she noticed a shimmering, toylike object in the ground. Her parents had told her time and time again not to pick up any dolls or toys from the ground. Nonetheless, her naive instincts took over. She immediately dove for the colorful bauble. It blew up, and both of Hawa's legs were nearly severed.

As a result of her misjudgment with the land mine she went through months of horrible pain and agony, but she would also suffer the loss of her legs for the rest of her life. She would have to learn how to get around without her limbs. Of course, she could get no real medical attention. There were few prosthetics available in the country, and a long waiting list for them. Further, the quality of the prosthetics was substandard and the sizes were often wrong.

Hawa grew more sympathetic to the other children she had seen who had also been disfigured by these land mines. Before, she had made fun of these scary-looking children. Their injuries ranged from a combination of loss of legs, feet, arms, and hands to holes blown in the face. She now associated herself with this group of victims and began to spend more time with them. They were too young to begin to understand the justification for the cruelty that they suffered; when they finally did understand, they were constantly reminded of the effect of Soviet aggression on their lives.

As Hawa grew up to become a beautiful young woman, she fell into deep cycles of depression over the loss of her legs. She felt that she did not deserve this kind of punishment. Hawa grew to loathe herself and became increasingly angry at the outside world. She watched in envy as other girls her age received marriage proposals from young men. She knew she had no prospects because of her handicap. Hawa would say, "Who wants to be with a girl who looks like me? How disgusting!" She also knew that her parents would not be alive forever to support and care for her. Without a husband, she would be left to live the rest of her life with her siblings or any other relatives who would be willing to take her in.

Eventually she fell in love with a young man, a distant relative who would visit her family from time to time. She could not possibly let him know how she felt. She only hoped that he would show some interest and return her feelings of attraction and admiration. But he never considered her, and eventually he became engaged to another girl. When Hawa learned of it, she immediately blamed it on her disfigured appearance. She plunged to the lowest point of depression and misery.

Two months after his engagement, she wrote a letter detailing the troubles of her life. She asked that nobody blame her for her actions, because she felt she had no choice in the matter. She set the letter aside, and then told her parents she was going to bathe. It was in the bathroom that she set herself on fire.

Countless Afghans fiercely resisted the Soviet invaders. As my family watched the slaughter from afar, we could take some comfort that these Afghans were dying for a meaningful cause, courageously resisting foreign aggression, but I was left to wonder what kind of justification that really was. Afghans were free citizens of a sovereign country. When had that fact come into question? How did the Soviet Union come up with the maniacal decision to try to force its Communist ideals on the free Afghan people? Why did

they think that they could subdue the Afghans, who had previously defeated all foreign forces that had attempted to take over
their country? As a girl, my mind raced with unanswered questions that seemed too simple and childish for such a large and complex problem. Yet I still have these questions, and they remain
unanswered.

The ranks of Afghanistan's Communist army withered significantly due to defections to the *mujahideen*. The mujahideen often
referred to themselves as "freedom fighters." They were people
from all walks of life who decided to place their homeland before
their lives. Given the powerful grip of the Soviets on their country,
they knew well that they stood no realistic chance of winning.
Since the mujahideen had emerged in reaction to the invasion,
they had no proper combat training or real preparation for the
battles they would engage in. They couldn't begin to compete with
the Soviet Union's level of sophistication, particularly in terms of
artillery. The Soviets had the latest weaponry and intelligence at
their disposal. What gave these Afghans, this group of ill-equipped
and ill-prepared people, the strength, confidence, and initiative to
attempt the impossible task of fighting head-to-head against a superpower?

Above all, Afghans never feel alone in the face of difficulty, as
they strongly believe that God is with them. If He willed it, then
all of the statistics and probabilities could be reversed. This ten-
dency to appeal to God is common for God-conscious Afghans,
who place their trust in nothing but God even in the face of life's
simplest obstacles. In the case of resisting the Soviet Union, it was
clear that nothing short of a miracle would allow them to break
free. It was also a matter of honor. They would never surrender
their dignity as a sovereign, self-governing people, and certainly
not to a foreign aggressor. Thus the mujahideen took to the battlefield with little chance that they would ever return alive.

The war did not consist of air strikes or other forms of techno-
logically advanced warfare but of face-to-face combat between

troops in fixed positions where they would either win or die. The Afghans did not engage in an all-out war in the commonly understood sense, such as by stopping enemy troops from entering the country. Instead, their strategy was to allow the Soviets to come right in with no resistance at all. Then they fired at them at night and destroyed their food and medical supplies, leaving them handicapped. According to some Russian journalists, a sizable portion of the costs of the war was due to the replacement food and supplies that had to be flown in constantly to the Russian soldiers. The Afghans simply tired out the Soviet soldiers, who complained that they would fight an entire village and think that they had taken it over, only to have to do the same thing again the next day. When the Soviets won positions, the Afghans retreated into the mountains and planned their next attack from there.

When I was old enough to begin to understand the war in Afghanistan, I started reading accounts of the Afghan mujahideen. I grew fascinated by the courage and nobility of these individuals who set aside their natural human instinct of self-preservation to defend their country and people. To most people, that's just a concept; witnessing the reality of it was overpowering. Those Afghans who would leave the comfort of their homes abroad to join the mujahideen were especially inspiring. One mujahid's words and experiences in particular influenced my outlook on life.

Yusuf was a full-time college student in Los Angeles, and he left his studies to join the mujahideen. His family begged him not to go, pleading with him to send money to support their cause instead, telling him that his presence there would not count for much among so many already fighting. But he felt an overwhelming need to defend his homeland, the place where he had grown up. He could not justify turning a blind eye to events there just because of the comforts he enjoyed in the United States. As he prepared to leave, I sensed that his state of mind was far above the "natural" preoccupations that I had grown accustomed to such as school, sports, movies, cars, and entertainment. I was a bit embarrassed about my priorities in contrast to his noble determination.

A few months later, Yusuf returned from Afghanistan alive. But he was changed, somber, having tasted the bitter realities of war. As he told me his story, a doorway to a new way of thinking opened for me. I had always been taught that each life is precious and valuable, and I certainly felt as though my individual life was of enormous value, not to be sacrificed for some greater good. Through him I was exposed to a new dimension of reality that was not "I-centered."

Yusuf told me of how the mujahideen sincerely and wholeheartedly left their homes and families to stand up to the Red Army. He told me of the numerous times that he faced what seemed certain death and yet somehow made it out alive. They entered the battlefield each day by kissing the Muslim holy book, the Quran, and shouting *"Allahu Akbar,"* "God is great!" These men fought tanks, helicopters, and sophisticated military planes with very little but their faithful zeal, yet they displayed no fear or regret on the battlefield. There was no question as to the validity of their cause in resisting the Communists. They believed that it was a fight between atheism and Islam—in other words, godlessness and godliness—and the principle of defending Islam from the atheist Communist doctrine in Afghanistan was faithfully upheld.

The mujahideen remained true to their five-times-daily prayer, and took extraordinary measures to pray even when they were in the battlefield. In the middle of the snow-capped mountains, the soldiers broke the ice-covered snow and entered it to cleanse themselves, performing the required ablution, or *wudu*, prior to prayer. Yusuf said that he felt as though his heart would stop from the cold when he washed in the snow in the freezing weather. Then they stood in straight lines to perform the prayer. But because they were always at risk of attack, each row took turns prostrating. This way, when one row was low on the ground and unable to see what lay before them, the other row, standing, could keep watch. Yusuf said that while food, water, clothing, shelter, family, and all other normalities of life had been sacrificed, the prayer could not be sacrificed. It was prayer that maintained their connection with God, sustained their hope, and gave them the focused energy and motivation to continue their resistance.

Yusuf talked a great deal about how God was on the side of the Afghans, and cited one incident that he said was the most powerful phenomenon he had ever seen. He was in a landlocked area where there was nothing but tall mountains surrounding him and his fellow mujahideen. Suddenly, some Soviet helicopters flew overhead and released a poisonous gas. The mujahideen watched as the cloud of gas slowly moved toward them. There was absolutely nothing they could do to escape. The men began to seek refuge in God and pray for help. Suddenly, it became gusty and very windy. The cloud of gas was briskly pushed away. Yusuf said that had he not seen it himself, he would not have believed such a story; but its truth remains permanently carved in his memory.

During Yusuf's months in the mountains, he watched his closest friends die. When he was himself injured and unable to move forward, he too was almost left to die. He was transformed by his experiences with the freedom fighters—as was I, though only through other peoples' accounts. Suddenly, the things that I took so seriously seemed trivial. I felt spiritually awakened, pulled out of my small view of the world into a grand view of life in which honor and self-respect are of the greatest importance.

❧ ❧

In the face of so much tribulation, the Afghan people have managed to develop a talent for maintaining their normality, sanity, and above all, their dignity. But one thing that still amazes me is the morale of the Afghans who continue to endure the hardships of living in their country. One finds these people in remarkably good spirits; they seem to have grown accustomed to their life circumstances—their attitude is that life simply must go on.

This is not to understate the real psychological trauma that has been inflicted upon them and the immense depression resulting from it, but to draw attention to their ability to cling to survival and contain the magnitude of their circumstances. I have encountered many people who have come from Afghanistan after living there for years facing death and destruction, and they seem remarkably in tune to appreciating and enjoying what really matters in life. Certainly they were not afflicted by the culture of consumption and wealth accumulation that plagues the people of my own society with another complex kind of depression.

A gentleman named Akbar stands out in my mind as the epitome of strength in the face of difficulty. Akbar and his wife decided to take their children and leave Afghanistan when death's shadow drew too near; their neighbors and close family members were falling victim to the war. No Afghan was permitted to leave the country, so they had to leave all of their savings in the bank in order not to arouse suspicion. They agreed with a smuggler to depart the following Friday evening, leaving their homes intact with all of their belongings, bringing only the clothes they wore. It was imperative that they travel by nightfall to conceal themselves from the enemy helicopters circling above that shot anything that moved below.

During the grueling trek through the dangerous mountains between Afghanistan to Pakistan, they reached extremely high elevations and could hardly see anything in front of them. Their smuggler guide warned them that there was absolutely nothing around them but the narrow road they walked on. If they slipped, they would fall down hundreds of feet of rocks. The children grew so sleepy that they couldn't continue any longer, but the smuggler insisted that they continue to walk the entire night so they could reach a relatively safer mark before the light of day.

The family carefully followed the narrow, winding path in a single-file line. The youngest of the boys, Tariq, straggled behind.

Tariq grew very weary and lost his balance, slipping off the side of the mountain and falling to his death.

Akbar nearly flung himself off the mountain to go after his little boy, but the smuggler held him back and angrily told him to restrain himself or lose his whole family. Any noise could attract attention to them and cause all of them to be killed on the spot. Akbar could do nothing but continue. He went into a state of shock. He felt as though he was having some kind of horrible nightmare.

They were more than halfway into the trip when their trusted smuggler pulled a gun on them and told them that he would kill them if they moved. They were stunned. They didn't know what to do, as this smuggler was their only hope for escaping the country alive. The smuggler then grabbed for Akbar's young girl, Nasreen. At that point, the entire family attacked the smuggler. The smuggler fired a single shot from his gun, instantly killing Akbar's only daughter, and then fled.

The family was crushed, devastated, and destroyed. Akbar carried his daughter's body, crying the entire time, until he finally found a place where they could bury her. They had no idea where to go; they just walked in what they thought was the right direction. Even if they were able to reach their destination, they knew they would have no recourse, no authorities to appeal to, no justice for what had just happened.

Upon finally arriving in Pakistan, Akbar underwent a humiliating and systematically racist process of harassment and exploitation. The corrupt Pakistani police, knowing he was Afghan, pressed him for bribes. He was forced to rent a house at a cost fifty percent higher than normal because he was Afghan, and the landlord demanded that he pre-pay the entire year's lease in cash. When Akbar asked the landlord why, he said that Afghans live in Pakistan only until they can make it to Germany or the U.S.; he might pick up and leave at any moment, and the landlord would lose money on the deal.

Akbar had used up almost all of his money to get out of Afghanistan in the first place, and certainly could not afford this. But the savvy landlord reminded him that most Afghans had relatives living abroad, especially in the United States. He said that he actually preferred U.S. dollars, as did most of the landlords in the area. So Akbar was pressured into calling his family in the U.S. and asking them to send him money so that he could afford shelter. In the meantime, he took his family to the camps that the Pakistani government had set up for Afghan refugees.

Akbar describes the camps as utterly devastating, not fit for animals to live in, let alone human beings. They amounted to nothing more than poor-quality tents with floors of bare ground. Often the dampness from the soil led to medical conditions. Disease was rampant because of the filth. But in the camps, Akbar was surprised to find the familiar faces of children of some of his friends from Afghanistan. The children told him that their parents had been killed on the journey into Pakistan, and now they had nowhere else to go but camps like this one. He was shocked to hear that his friends had died and to see their lovely children, who were once so pampered by their adoring parents, now living in such revolting conditions. "It made my heart bleed," says Akbar.

Akbar was tried and tested in every way, but remarkably he and other Afghans rose above their misfortunes. He eventually made it to the United States and worked diligently to build a life for his family. He thanked God each day for the opportunity to live, as he had known so many others who had died along the way. He savored the little pleasures of life. He never argued about petty things with his wife; such things were beneath them. His children appreciated the family that remained to them, and they remained true to their cultural principles of loyalty and honor.

When I asked Akbar how he managed to keep his sanity through these difficult years of his life, he said it was because he was lucky enough never to lose his honor and dignity—the only thing, he said, that can destroy the true Afghan. He said that he stayed in his country as long as he could, and did not leave it until his family's life was in real danger. He never traded his homeland for wealth and comfort, but left only when he had no other choice. He thanks God that the daughter he lost was not dishonored by that smuggler, and that even though she died, she did not lose her dignity.

Akbar seemed to look on the bright side of the darkest and most difficult situations, and he appealed to God through everything. He said that the Afghans were being tested by God, that there was a point to all of this, that it did not happen for no reason, and that they must rise to the occasion by showing their strength, perseverance, and patience. Interestingly enough, when I mentioned to him how unfortunate it was that we would certainly never see peace in Afghanistan during our lifetimes, he smiled and said, "God has always come to our aid. We rely on Him alone to deliver us, and are sure without a doubt that He will accept our prayers."

Living comfortably in the States, I often felt guilty for some of the luxuries that I enjoyed, as I knew that deserving people were deprived in Afghanistan. Girls who were better than me, who dealt with so much more difficulty and never made a fuss over it, couldn't take a hot shower, enjoy a really great meal, or have the opportunity to think about something creative, fun, or naughty — they had to think only of basic survival. During the Soviet war, when I took a shower, at the end of it I would turn the water temperature all the way to cold so that I could stay in touch with what others felt like. Sometimes, during the hot, smoggy San Fernando Valley summers, I would turn off the air conditioner so that I would not indulge too much in comforts that others could not even hope for.

❧ ❧

When the Soviets invaded Afghanistan, the sight of tanks in the once-peaceful streets and the mere thought of Russia's tight grip on the country caused many in our family to cry like children.

They felt they had no hope of defending themselves against a monster of this size and capability. Indeed, many Afghans admit to me that they did not even entertain the thought that they could break loose from the Soviet grip. Looking back, they say it was miraculous that they actually won the war and regained their autonomy.

One Afghan gentleman, Ayub, told me, "How we freed ourselves from the KGB, how we broke loose from that dreaded Red Army, how we escaped the venomous threat of Communism—it's simply beyond me. When they invaded, I thought our fate, the fate of the Afghans, had been sealed just as it had been for President Daoud Khan. When he cut his trip to Russia short after Brezhnev accused him of becoming too close with the U.S., he was killed by Soviet-backed insurgents almost exactly one year later. It seemed that as they signed his death warrant, they signed the death warrant of the entire nation." Ayub continued, "I cannot attribute the credit for this victory to ourselves, not to our ability or strength or anyone else's. It is enough to concede that someone was watching over us from above, and I thank God that we Afghans must have done something right for God Almighty to take mercy on us."

The Afghans fought the Soviets at a great price. But they also proved to be a people who would sacrifice everything to defend and protect their principles. They felt that their sacrifice would be well worth the later, more valuable gain of independence. And it was. After a decade of unsuccessful battle, Soviet Premier Mikhail Gorbachev said that Afghanistan had become a "bleeding wound" for his country and decided to withdraw his troops. Soon after, the Soviet Union unraveled entirely.

In addition to the personal qualities and ingenious strategies of the freedom fighters, some important external factors helped Afghanistan claim this miraculous victory. First, Afghanistan's terrain includes some of the highest elevations in the world and is very difficult to penetrate physically. Many analysts have described the country as having a natural fortress built around it. One Russian general said in frustration, "It is like God took all of the rocks in the world and placed them in Afghanistan!" Second, the U.S. government generously supplied arms to the mujahideen. The U.S. did not commit support in the initial stages of the war, so Afghans were the ones who took the initiative in the resistance; but when the U.S. began giving aid to the mujahideen, it allowed the fight to continue and led more people to join the Afghan forces.

The mujahideen's cause was so worthy that even non-Afghans joined it. But unfortunately, as soldiers died and were replaced by new recruits, their forces started to become diluted with a different brand of so-called mujahideen who were in fact nothing but common thieves and thugs. The principle-based warriors were nearly exterminated over the years, and their good name became abused by these latecomer profiteers who terrorized their own people in the state of lawlessness and chaos that the war created. This group of people was ruthless and mercilessly took advantage of Afghan civilians. Young girls were kidnapped, common citizens were hustled for money, and men were killed for the most trivial of reasons. In essence, they were a kind of mafia that dominated its turf by exercising its ability to brutalize those who did not cooperate. In turn, they transformed the name "mujahideen" from one that represented freedom fighters to one that inspired feelings of disgust. Worse, they brought forth a generation of hardened children raised on hatred and anger who knew nothing but war and destruction. They were fuel for the fire of civil war that was to come.

When the Soviets left, the U.S. and the rest of the world turned away, focusing their interest on other priorities. Meanwhile, Afghanistan was left in shambles. Warlords who emerged from within the new circle of corrupted mujahideen took advantage of the lawless state of the country. It became a haven for a black-market bazaar of arms, sport utility vehicles, drugs, and any other commodity in demand. There was no governmental control. This lawlessness meant that virtually anyone could come into Afghanistan and do as they pleased—which is what Al Qaeda ended up doing. There was no one to document those who entered the country. A survival-of-the-fittest social scheme began to take root. Those who had the physical or monetary force to stay on top held their own. Most people, who were peaceful and had only enough money to maintain their daily lives, were ravaged.

Another dangerous phenomenon that arose during the Soviet war was the birth of Afghan political factions, or *hezb*. These factions represented the major ethnic groups within the country. Each faction received funding from different countries and incorporated their sponsoring countries' interests into their own agendas. This dynamic allowed Afghanistan to be manipulated by foreign countries like a giant game of chess, to the country's further ruin.

Although Communism presumably intended to destroy all ideas of ethnicity in favor of a system that built unity based on economic class, tribalism began making a comeback during the Soviet occupation. Maybe it was because Communism never delivered the economic wealth it promised, or because Afghan Communists were divided into different sects based on language, location, and ideology. Whatever the cause, it incited the different tribes of Afghans to racial discrimination, hatred, and murder. After the Soviet withdrawal, the country plunged into a horrific civil war, which was led and fought by the various political factions. Countless lives were lost in a struggle over who would control the country. The ethnic factions multiplied and fueled a civil war that lasted as long as the Soviet war, fostering deep animosity among the ethnic groups of the country.

Afghanistan is a salad bowl of ethnicities that retains the identity of each group, rather than a melting pot that recycles them all into one new homogenous identity. However, a sense of oneness is found among the different peoples through the country's music, literature, arts, and religion of Islam. My parents tell me that when they were going to school in Afghanistan, they were not conscious of others' ethnic or religious backgrounds, and held no grudge against the nation's diverse ethnic groups. My mom says that some of her closest school friends were Shiite Muslims (Sunni is dominant in Afghanistan), but that she never knew about it until the fact came up by chance decades later in America. It wasn't that people hid their identities or kept them secret; it was just not a question of interest to people. They had never known the kind of violent tribalism that surfaced after the Soviet withdrawal.

This is not to say that the people of Afghanistan bear no responsibility for the tribalism. Afghans have engaged in many skirmishes along ethnic lines. Each group tries to prove its superiority over the other in some fashion, whether it be racial heritage, language, looks, physical superiority, or character traits. There was never a deep unity among the different kinds of Afghans. When Afghans are asked why they aren't more unified, they point their fingers at one another. The Farsi speakers, or *Farsi-Zubans*, say that they have been systematically discriminated against by the majority Pashtuns, who have always favored their own people and swayed the social distribution of goods to their side. Pashtuns argue that they have no prejudice against the Farsi-speaking Afghans, but are unfairly blamed for their problems due to an inferiority complex.

Interestingly, it is not primarily ethnicity but the languages of Farsi and Pashto that are the main divider among Afghans. Afghans perceive language differences as indicators of a person's behavior and conduct. The *Pashto-Zubans*, or Pashto-speaking tribes, have become characterized as a certain type of people, and the Farsi-Zubans have been branded as another. For example, it is generally thought that Pashtuns are simpler and less sophisticated than Farsi-Zubans. According to these stereotypical notions, Pashtuns are warlike people who do not solve problems with intellect or reasonable argument. Rather, they lash out in a violent verbal or physical manner, "winning" an argument by overpowering their opponents with might rather than by being truly right.

But Pashtuns view these simple qualities as sincere, honest, and genuine. They believe that unlike Farsi-Zubans, they are real people who are clear about their intentions and feelings, whereas Farsi-Zubans will smile in your face and stab you in the back. They feel that Farsi speakers like to boast about their modernity and their supposedly more civilized, Westernized social behavior, because they have freed themselves from many traditional constraints that Pashtuns continue to uphold. They see Farsi speakers as believing themselves to be more complex than Pashtuns, able to foresee situations to take advantage of Pashtuns. They will not allow themselves to be fooled by anyone; if anything, they will be the ones doing the fooling. The unconditionally kindhearted and straight-shooting approach of Pashtuns can get them into trouble when not met with the same kind of gestures; it leaves them open to those who will capitalize on their sincerity with insincerity.

Farsi-Zubans who buy into these stereotypes enjoy a sense of superiority over their "old-fashioned" Pashtun counterparts. Closed-minded Pashtuns, on the other hand, look down on Farsi-Zubans for their weak-willed and gilded outlook on life. The relationship between these conceptions are analogous to how urban Californians or New Yorkers and rural Texans or Southerners view each other.

Pashtuns make up a large ethnic majority of Afghanistan's population, and generally held power in the country historically. Even if a ruler no longer spoke Pashto because he had lived in the city for a long time and had grown accustomed to speaking Farsi, he identified himself with his Pashtun heritage. The least-powerful ethnic groups are the Farsi speakers, generally Hazara, Tajik, or Uzbek. They come from the minority northern areas that have taken control of the country since the events of 2001.

Before the Soviet invasion, some ethnic groups had been systematically held down, such as the Eastern-featured Hazaras. These Afghans, who are primarily Shiite Muslims, essentially composed the servant class of the country. During my stay at my grandparents' home in Kabul, I experienced a kind of culture shock at their practice of keeping servants. A maid's quarters was located in the far corner of my grandparents' backyard, where a family of Hazaras lived in exchange for household service. The servants had a daughter named Sakina who would run to the grocery store to bring my mother cigarettes as well as my own favorite treat, a fabulous-tasting orange gum that came in small white boxes. I noticed that Sakina did a lot of work around the house and I wondered why she, who was only about thirteen years old, did so much work rather than playing.

I became accustomed to Sakina and her family being around, but one day I came home and their quarters were vacant. Sakina and I had become playmates, and I was sad that she was gone and confused about why she and her family had left. My grandmother explained to me that my grandfather had gotten angry with them for cutting the grass without permission. The yard had looked very green; now that they had cut it, the ugly, yellow dead grass had become exposed. Just like that, they were forced to move out without notice and to find another employer to live with. I felt very bad about the way these Hazaras were treated, because I did not view them as being different from me.

This mistreatment of Hazaras fostered a great deal of aggression, which they must have harbored for a very long time. Any degree of coexistence and tolerance that existed before the Soviet occupation was stripped away during the civil war, during which Hazaras brutalized the Pashtuns of the south to avenge past crimes. Hatred also erupted between Sunnis and Shiites. Though the Shiites were a small minority of the population, their political faction gained representation, and with their new power they too grew ruthless. The Hazaras also gained political representation through their own independent faction, but it became an obstacle to freedom and equality rather than a boost toward that end, since the political factions provided a form of systematic, licensed killing rather than actual political representation. Despite their leaders' professed goals, the factions' behavior was based more on power and greed than on justice.

All of the political faction leaders are multimillionaires who live incredibly comfortable lives compared to the poor Afghan citizens who struggle to make it through each day. As long as foreign powers supplied these factions with arms and cash, they stubbornly fought at the cost of many people's lives. During the civil war, the wealthy faction leaders lived abroad, never in Afghanistan—with one exception. Ahmad Shah Masoud, the late leader of the Northern Alliance, lived in the Panjshir, or Five Lions Valley, during the war. His geographical position gave him isolation, and his part of the country remained independent even during the rule of the Taliban.

The civil war was swept away when the Taliban gained control of most of the country, with the exception of regions controlled by the Northern Alliance. While the Afghan political factions gawked at the fact that the rug had been pulled from beneath them by an unknown entity, the Taliban fulfilled the basic need for people to gain some form of safety and security from the devastation of the Soviet and civil wars.

Years later, in the 2001 summit in Bonn, Germany, during the election and appointment of the new Afghan government, a taste of the old struggles was evident between various faction leaders who worked to gain as much representation in the new government as possible. Following the summit meetings, the former Afghan president, Borhanuddin Rabbani, tried to renegotiate his piece of the pie by saying that he had caved to international pressure and that he should actually be entitled to more governmental representation. Finally, in June 2002, an ethnically balanced cabinet was formed by the new elected head of state, President Hamid Karzai.

In the beginning of this government-building process, the United Nations grew impatient that Afghanistan's leadership was not taking on the cookie-cutter shape of most governments. But

Afghanistan's government cannot be expected to conform to what most governments look like. How many other governments have used the *loya jirga* method, in which all the various ethnicities are represented—and more importantly, how many have worked under such a method? The country is unique on almost all levels and must be understood relative to its own setting, not in reference to other paradigms.

When the Soviet war ended, the brief elation of victory was soon followed by deep disappointment. From their safe havens abroad, refugee Afghans lamented that their countrymen, who had so bravely and incredibly defeated the Soviet invaders, had now turned their guns on one another. Their hopes of returning home were dashed, and their need to press on with assimilating into the societies of their adoptive countries became more evident. Indeed, it was hard even for American-born Afghans like me not to connect our own struggles with the struggles that were going on "over there." I personally felt that every problem I faced could be traced directly to the historical accidents that plagued Afghanistan. In this atmosphere a new breed of Afghans pioneered and cultivated its identity, one that became known as the *Afghan-American*.

～ Four ～

Growing Up Muslim Afghan-American

I am very grateful for my experiences in America. Had I lived in Afghanistan during the past two decades of war, I am not sure I would be alive today, let alone writing a book and working on a PhD at a prestigious private university. My family and I have been afforded a wealth of opportunities here. While I diligently endeavor to become a college professor, my sister has earned her bachelor's degree and plans to begin graduate studies next year, and my brother plows forward in his undergraduate work with hopes of one day going to law school and entering government service.

We are living the lives that my parents had always dreamed for us. When I told my dad that I had been accepted to the PhD program at the University of Southern California (USC), he was floored, even as he sat in a boardroom meeting with the owners and vice presidents of his company. When he calmed down, he quietly told me that he would call me back in a few minutes. Apparently his overwhelming response caused his colleagues to stop the meeting, so he excused himself. When he called me back, he told me, "You have made my life. I could die today and have no regrets."

To those who have not struggled through the difficulties of immigrant life and have not seen what life is like under more unfavorable circumstances, American life can seem pretty banal, even full of personal voids. Getting accepted to graduate or law school might seem like normal routine for many Americans in their twenties, but not for my family. We are part of the first generation of Afghans to be born in the United States, and we are pioneering the future of generations of Afghan-Americans to come.

If we had grown up in Afghanistan during the past two decades, our future would not be so bright. All that would await us is heartache and grief from death, starvation, loss of livelihood, and destruction of our psyches. Although Afghan life was not always as grim as it is today, it is the worst memories that stand out most vividly. Afghanistan is a broken nation full of heartbroken people. Even during its peaceful years, only the people of Kabul and exceptionally wealthy merchants were privileged to live a life of ease and comfort. They represented a very small slice of the country. Most of the population lived a painfully difficult and grueling lifestyle. I cannot even begin to imagine where we would be if my parents had not made the rebellious decision to move to America.

However, I am not simply an American. I am an Afghan-American. Following September 11, I noticed many who felt that the hyphenated American was a hoax, a ruse to allow "foreigners" to reap the benefits of America while their allegiance lay with their native countries. I heard many people, both in person and on television, disgusted at the fact that the suicide hijackers had come to the United States, gained educations from American universities, and learned how to fly in U.S. flight schools, only to turn around and use their training against this country. Their behavior was somehow projected onto Muslims as a whole. On television I saw a mosque in Texas surrounded by protesters who vehemently yelled, "Go home, you don't deserve to be here!" One protestor said, "All they do is take advantage of our opportunities and freedoms, while they continue to hate us and devise ways of destroying us!" On talk shows, such as Bill Maher's "Politically Incorrect," others have said that all the ethnic groups that now exist in America—African, Japanese, Irish, Italian, and so on—have at some point paid their dues by enduring the burden of being the new kids on the block, and now it is the turn of Muslim Middle Easterners. In other words, the regrettable way we treat each new immigrant group needs no justification other than that since it occurred in the past, it should blindly recur in the future.

But clearly, the *ideals* of America are graciously welcoming of new peoples, and confer equality without prejudice. America does not even impose a melting-pot social scheme where people of various cultures must meld into one new identity. Rather, the salad bowl of varying flavors and cultures is widely accepted. For the most part, each group can maintain its own identity, language, and so forth without being viewed as any less American—in fact, it makes them seem more substantive and cultured. We are not forced to simply leave our heritage and civilization behind, but can rather create a synthesis of old and new experiences to improve upon and actualize ourselves. Although those who are hateful and ignorant will try to prove otherwise, it is in fact the wisdom and richness of other cultures and languages that significantly contribute to the fabric of this society.

It was through the experience of living and being raised in the United States that I came to truly appreciate and understand my own religion, heritage, culture, and language. As my peers strove to find themselves and searched for some type of connection to their identity, I found my rich and powerful background and embraced it. While some who have emigrated from Eastern countries have decisively lost their cultural values, I have been on a constant quest to delve further into them and to connect with my roots. This has added a great deal of flavor to my life. I feel that my experiences in America have allowed me to own my heritage and truly be the person I am.

There are few other countries that protect civil liberties with guarantees as strong as those found in our Constitution and Bill of Rights. However, through experience, I have learned that there will always be close-minded and radical people in every society. Both the West and the East have their fair share. The only way to combat the darkness of ignorance is with the light of knowledge. This is the main reason I have decided to enter the field of education. It is only through a process of genuinely understanding each other that we will be able to bridge the gaps peacefully and avoid wars, bloodshed, and destruction.

Ignorance is a plague that infects all peoples and societies regardless of race, religion, creed, or socioeconomic status. It affects all people. While some radical Muslims may believe that to be American is un-Islamic, these are individual opinions that are not supported by the religion of Islam. According to Islam, the entire universe was created by God. He did not specify patches of the world as good or bad. It is all God's earth, and people are free to dwell upon it as they please. Furthermore, Islam transcends all cultural and geographical boundaries. As the Quran states, "We have created you into nations and tribes so that you may recognize each other, not that you might despise one another" (49:13).

❧ ☙

I was the child of an Afghan couple who couldn't go back to visit their country for decades. I led a life that was split clearly in half between at home and outside of home. These two worlds were separated only by my front door, yet they were so different that it seemed they couldn't be reconciled. As a first-generation Afghan-American girl born and raised in Los Angeles, I felt, quite unconsciously, that the only way I could assimilate with my more "mainstream" peers would be to move as far away as possible from my confining Afghan self. American and Afghan cultures are so disparate that there seemed to be no hope for marrying the two. This left only one choice, to shift completely toward one value system or the other.

My Afghan self encompassed more than just my appearance. It was entrenched in me: in my language, which impacted the way I thought; in my family, and how they fit into society at large; and in my mannerisms, demeanor, mores, and principles. I'm sure most of my friends would insist that I had been just as well adjusted and socially assimilated as any other teenage girl in my social position. But I was very conscious of my "failing" self—that is, my Afghan self as I perceived it in accordance with the "failing" state of Afghanistan—at all times. The pressure was very real to me, and at this stage of my life, I couldn't simply shake it off and claim not to care. My human need to fit in, heightened by my youth, forced me to care. Yet I couldn't articulate this need, nor did I fully realize its presence at that time.

I found that I couldn't fully and comfortably fit into either the Afghan community or the mainstream American society, despite my efforts to do so. According to my fellow Afghans who had been born in Afghanistan, I was a hyphenated Afghan, an "Afghan-American." That set me apart from the true and authentic Afghans, who merely resided in America. But my Afghan features—deep tan skin, bold green eyes, full lips, and strong bone structure—were a constant reminder that I did not belong to American society in the way most others did. Unlike some of my foreign-born peers, I couldn't "pass" for white even if I wanted to.

In school I had been taught the American ideals of equality and liberty for all. I was well aware that they should make me just as much an American as everyone else. However, these ideals simply did not match my actual experiences. Of course, I faced teasing—being called a sand nigger, being asked if my uncle was Saddam Hussein, and all sorts of other blatant, shameless attacks on my self. Looking back I see these experiences as silly and childish, certainly nothing to be taken to heart. But at that time, I felt the impact of those words deeply, regardless of my witty retorts or ability to pretend if even to myself that they didn't affect me.

My religious beliefs set me apart even further. I didn't want to violate my religious moral principles, which were incompatible with the usual lifestyle of mainstream American youth. I was prohibited from partaking in the normal social events that would include a school dance, my high school prom, or other school-related activities—not even with girlfriends, and certainly not with a male date.

Islam forbids drinking, dating in the commonly understood sense of the term, physical contact between males and females prior to marriage, and so forth. These elements of Islam, which are also found in other religions, did not mesh with the life of a "normal" teenager. I accepted these principles and had internalized them to the extent that I couldn't turn my back on them. I really believed in these moral codes. If I did participate in what everyone else was doing, I couldn't enjoy it as others did, because I would be spiritually accountable for those transgressions. My conscience held me back. But I was able to deal with the Islamic part of my identity; it was the cultural aspect that felt cumbersome, because it was so critical of my Islamic consciousness.

When I acquired an Islamic consciousness during my late adolescence, a desire to strive for God's favor is what drove me to do the morally correct thing. Islam gave me a kind of inner-directedness that dictated my conduct. But even when Afghan children are not in touch with Islam, their cultural constraints quickly teach them to behave in accordance with certain conservative protocols, to guard their own and their family's reputations. This kind of morality is based heavily on social approval and other-directedness.

If an Afghan child decides to do something that is not socially accepted by Afghans, they are told not to do it on the grounds of "What will people think?" They are raised with a code of morality that is based on gaining favorable public opinion, or at least not attracting negative opinion. But this kind of thinking can lead to a double life when a person is straddling two cultures. I noticed that many Afghan youths who seemed "innocent" and "cultured" in front of adults were leading other lives behind the scenes. They followed the expected behaviors at home but violated them as they pleased when they were outside of Afghan social circles. The key was to maintain a perfect reputation, which could easily be done while carrying on a life of drinking, premarital or extramarital sex, and so forth, on the side.

As they grow old enough to go to college, young Afghans find themselves being steered away from the behavioral sciences and into professions such as engineering or medicine, which are considered to be more prestigious. Teaching is also viewed as an honorable career path, though more suited for women as far as more traditional Afghans are concerned, unless at the university level. Some might disregard what others think, but most Afghans are trained to care about and internalize these principles to the point that they will desire what they have been taught is desirable.

Afghan girls are supposed to dress conservatively, be polite, and above all maintain their innocence. What is meant by innocence? According to Afghan tradition, a girl must maintain her verbal, emotional, and physical innocence. She must refrain from speech that reveals that she has been exposed to undesirable situations. She is to keep her mind off boys, sex, drugs, and alcohol, and on her education and family.

Under no circumstances is it acceptable for her to lose her virginity prior to marriage. In past generations, a beautiful white cloth would be placed on the bed of the bride and groom with the expectation that it would be stained with blood the morning after the wedding night. If it were not, the bride was cursed and sent back to her parents' home in disgrace. Nowadays, although the white-sheet practice has been abandoned, a traditional Afghan girl must still give her husband assurance that she is pure. It is yet another example of the kind of acceptance and approval that must be gained from people rather than from God to maintain personal dignity.

According to some Muslims, such obedience to other human beings constitutes a form of associating partners with God, or *shirk* in Arabic, because it drives people to obey the dictates of people rather than the Creator. It also poses a double standard. Males of the community are neither required to prove their chastity nor expected to adhere to the same standards as girls. Guys who engage in drinking alcohol, sex, and nightclubbing are usually dismissed with a "boys will be boys" attitude and are not shunned in the community like girls are. This double standard, however, does not apply to the more religious Afghans, who frown upon such behavior regardless of gender.

Intermixing with the opposite sex is a highly sensitive area for Afghans who view it as wrong. Many Afghan youths my age had difficulty meeting each other because of the social hesitation to allow them to mingle freely at weddings or other social gatherings. In Islam, a man and woman are allowed to speak to each other and see each other in order to decide whether their relationship has a future and can lead to marriage. But according to the Afghan code, if one is discovered doing that, especially if that person is a girl, she becomes marked. And when these meetings do not result in any kind of long-term future, as is naturally often the case, then the girl is even more ostracized because she is seen as loosely trying everyone out.

In high school it is natural for boys and girls to begin to take an interest in one another, but the Afghan youth had to conceal these interests, so that they appeared nonexistent. Feelings of this nature were inconceivable, not subject to open or forthright conversation and certainly not made public. My own attempts toward assimilation were always curtailed by my father's insistence that I lead an "Afghan" life. Even when I attempted to replace the school affairs with Islamic events such as youth camps and other fun yet religiously oriented trips, I was held back from them because of my father's insistence that a good Afghan girl wouldn't go traveling on her own commingled with boys. Certainly, people would talk and wonder if I was "modernizing" the Islam that they knew.

I sometimes envied my Persian girlfriends, whose society has become quite open in recent years. There was a nice balance between maintaining conservative ideals and being understanding. One such friend, Shiva, was able to bring Persian boys to family gatherings and introduce them as her "friends." They were seen as cute, and in fact they really were just friends who happened to share a puppy-love attraction. Her social circles understood this, and so, although she professed that she would certainly marry a particular boy one day, nobody frowned upon her or was shocked when it didn't happen despite her best intentions.

Shiva was able to talk about the boys at school she had a crush on with her family, and she was given loads of advice on how to handle them. By the time she got married, Shiva had grown experienced in the positive sense of the term—she had been through enough platonic yet mature relationships that she knew what type of person she ought to marry and how to navigate through her marriage. This was and continues to be unheard of in Afghan society, even in America. In Afghan circles, when two people are interested in one another, they can exchange glances across the room if they both happen to be invited to the same social gathering; at best they can talk outside when no one else is around. There is a very sneaky and deceptive component to relationships that are not officiated. Of course, *how* people actually get to know each other well enough to start an officiated relationship is overlooked.

Still, though Shiva seemed to have it pretty good, I must have seemed lucky to those Afghans who came to the U.S. later on. Children of Afghan refugees were often burdened with helping to support their families financially. They sacrificed studying and childhood amusements to bear these adult responsibilities. They grew up in rough housing projects or other low-income communities and became intent on making quick money however possible. This resulted in a crop of youth who were violent, rebellious, uneducated, and angry. It was not long before gangs dominated the streets wherever Afghan girls and boys took pride in their war-waging abilities. Afghan gangs have become particularly infamous in Northern California for their harsh brand of violence. The gulf between Afghan generations deepened as parents remained in sheltered lives and their children toughed it out in the real world for them. There were those who made the adjustment despite difficult circumstances, but they were exceptions. While children turning to gangs was an extreme case, certainly their prospects for a prosperous future were systematically limited.

These differences among the various Afghans I knew were invisible to me when I was a young girl. I viewed all Afghans equally, regardless of their socioeconomic status or ethnic background. So for many years I remained baffled at why I simply could not adjust to their norms. I felt isolated from these young Afghans. I didn't speak Farsi as well as they did, so we couldn't properly communicate. I didn't dress as they did or share their interests. They were beginning new lives in a foreign country, but this country had always been my home. They struggled through ESL courses as I busily worked my way through a magnet program for gifted students that was attended by mainstream girls and boys, even though I was always the only Afghan among them.

But my semblance of normality was hardly complete, as I couldn't do many of the things everyone else did. I was not allowed to go to birthday parties or other such functions held outside of school. I couldn't keep in contact with my friends after school on a consistent basis except on the telephone. Above all, I felt as though my peers were always conscious of my foreign physical appearance. I didn't have the same blonde hair or fair skin.

I could not escape this constant awareness. Attention was always drawn to the differences between our lifestyles in subtle, tacit ways. It was embedded in the language people used: "How do *you guys* . . ." It was always *us* guys versus *you* guys. Once I joined some girlfriends at a restaurant for a birthday (with my father's permission, as it was during the day). Our group was chaperoned by one friend's mother. The mother asked me if the reason I ate so slowly had to do with how I was taught to be as a

Muslim or Afghan girl. I realize that the intention of her comment did not stem from prejudice, but most likely from simple curiosity. Nonetheless, this example stands out in my mind in terms of how it reinforced my identity in terms of my physical appearance. My appearance served as a constant reminder that I was in fact an outsider, and therefore had to justify and explain my behavior relative to my religious or social background rather than relative to just being me.

In the ninth grade, after trying to ignore, suppress, and annihilate these issues during the critical years of life when people are programmed to desire social acceptance, it became painfully clear that I could not find this acceptance anywhere in my environment. I accepted that I would never be the same as everyone else and surrendered my resistance to this notion. I finally came to terms with the fact that I never would be totally accepted in white American circles despite how "tolerant" everyone was. I did not want to be "tolerated." This realization caused a major shift in my ideals, and it drove me to find ways to be true to my "real" identity.

This was the year I decided to undertake my first observation of fasting for the Islamic month of Ramadan. According to the Islamic calendar, this was the month when the Quran, the Islamic holy book, was revealed. My paternal grandmother had encouraged me to practice the fast ever since I had become mature enough to handle it and understand its true meaning. She had moved to the U.S. six years earlier, and played a crucial role in shaping my Afghan and Muslim identity.

My grandmother explained Ramadan to me as a way of purifying both the physical and spiritual selves. By not eating or drinking from sunrise to sunset, I would gain a true perspective of how the poor and starving feel. It was also a practice of mind over matter, because I would have to gain control over my physical desires.

But the most challenging part of fasting for me did not have to do with abstaining from food and drink. The hardest part was restraining my temper and refraining from ill-mannered conduct. Although many Muslims reduce the fast to just matters of eating and drinking, in fact we are supposed to engage in a full fast that requires controlling all of our senses. We should not look at anything immoral; engage in speech that is destructive, hurtful, or in any way lewd or rude; or physically touch anything that is impermissible, so that all parts of the body and senses are equal participants in the fast. For a know-it-all teenager with a bratty set of siblings, being patient and good-tempered was the most difficult demand of all.

Yet somehow, and somewhat amazingly, I did it. And doing it made me feel spiritually uplifted and open to the real meaning of life. Rather than focusing on the small circumstances of my own life, I began to develop an inclination to look at the larger scheme of things. The fasting made me feel as though I had been sleepwalking through my life before. This awakening touched every part of my being. But it also confirmed for me that I would never be able to go back to the way I had lived before.

My newfound enthusiasm for my heritage and religion impelled me to begin writing editorials for the school newspaper to dispel misconceptions about Islam. It was not too long before I founded a Muslim Student Association (MSA) at my high school. There had been no high-school-based MSAs before it, so I didn't have much to model it on. But there were many Muslims in my school who were eager to help in the effort.

Many people were surprised that a Muslim girl could lead an Islamic organization, particularly since most of the active members were boys. In fact, most of the Muslims at my high school were boys and seemed to be more inclined toward participating in the MSA than the girls. Though girls would sometimes attend, they would cite various reasons for not being regular members, such as the speakers being too boring or not enough other girls attending. Eventually I noticed that in most of my dealings with other MSAs, even throughout college, I was often the only girl in a leadership position.

The nature of adolescence is to be idealistic and emotional about one's causes. Thus I would always encounter one or two passionate young people in the group who would try to render virtually everything unlawful and sinful. Strangely enough, these were the members I shared the best relationships with. They were the "hard core" guys, and they would nominate me and vote me into leadership throughout my MSA experiences from high school to college. I had always tried very hard to maintain my respectability among the boys and to avoid being taken lightly. Being accepted by these more zealous members confirmed to me that I was doing something right, because they were more likely than anyone to be critical. It was through my involvement with the local MSAs that I became known in the community. Eventually, I noticed my dad introducing himself in local social circles as "Maryam's father." I just loved that! I never expressed my love to my parents verbally, but rather did so through winning their pride and confidence.

In coordinating activities for the MSA, I had to deal more with teachers and school administrators, and I soon realized the extent of their ignorance about Islam. The school authorities were totally unaware of even the basics. They didn't know that Islam is one of the great monotheistic religions, along with Christianity and Judaism. Islam was seen as a kind of mystical and strange way of life, not expected to be practiced by anyone who was broad-minded, educated, or normal. When I told them that Islam is one of the Abrahamic faiths and that it encompassed all of the prophets, including Jesus, Moses, Noah, Jacob, and Joseph (peace be upon them), they were totally surprised. It was strange to me that Islam could be so misunderstood, especially when I had read that it was the fastest-growing religion in the world.

Even though I had always been a Muslim before, it had been more in name than in practice. I now felt a surge of will to revert to the authentic teachings of the religion of Islam. This authentic version must be distinguished from the commonly understood version—which had been grossly distorted by both Muslims and non-Muslims out of ignorance, a desire to mold the religion to fit personal desires, or outright hatred of it.

People who hate Islam are not all outside the Muslim faith. Many Muslims themselves have bought into the stereotypes and misconceptions of the religion, and have become self-loathing as a result. It was a strange contradiction: All around me I found Afghans and Muslims of other cultures who were very proud of their Muslim identity and who would fight anyone who tried to bash or degrade it; yet their faith was like an empty shell, not grounded in any kind of real sacrifice. We were all Muslims, but none of us observed or practiced the true essence of the religion, and in fact we poked fun at those who did for being zealous or hypocritical.

Practicing Muslims were constantly tested for their sincerity. If a devout Muslim claimed to be "religious," the nonpracticing Muslims immediately jumped to ask obvious questions about covering hair, praying, listening to music, dancing, and so on. These were all ways to judge another person's claim to faith and to point out that their quality of faith was poor and disingenuous. Those who actually were religious were deemed to be fake or false simply because they may not have adhered to certain practices.

This system of debasing religious members of the community generally occurred only among younger people. The elderly were expected to be religious as a matter of cultural tradition. Elders are normally seen praying five times a day and adhering to all the Islamic codes of conduct that they disregarded in their youth. Perhaps this is because as death approaches, we look to the hereafter and sense a need for repentance. But when I first began to discover and embrace Islam, I didn't recognize that negative mentality that existed among my Afghan peers.

According to Islam, one element of being a true Muslim, and specifically a true Muslim woman, is to cover one's hair and to dress conservatively by not wearing revealing clothing. The purpose of this conservative dress is to eliminate the social issues that arise from sexuality, as well as to promote modesty. Men must also dress conservatively in society, and are to conduct themselves respectfully with women. Both men and women are taught by the Quran to lower their gazes in public, maintaining their modesty at all times. Chastity goes hand in hand with modesty. It is an important obligation on Muslims to guard their chastity, and it is believed that modesty keeps one away from the steps that lead to unchaste behavior. During my sophomore year in high school, I joyously plunged into the practice of covering my hair with the hijab and dressing conservatively.

I had not expected to receive too many stares, glares, and awkward looks as a result of my decision to put a simple piece of cloth around my hair. I thought it would probably not be as big a deal as the hype made it sound. Little did I know what I was getting myself into. Shortly after I began to wear the Islamic dress, in 1991, President George H. W. Bush led the country into the Gulf War against Iraq. The war brought with it a flurry of anti-Semitism—hatred of those of Middle Eastern descent—and specifically anti-Islamic sentiment.

Since Saddam was the new enemy, I suppose everyone who was a member of his cultural or religious group had to pay. At school, students would shout "F—— Islam!" after me. Others would call me the "ninja lady" or "camel jockey." I was also called a "towel head," which actually alluded to members of the Sikh religion, whose men cover their hair with turbans. I tried not to react to these insults because I was restrained by Islamic principles. However, my best friend, Sara, was outraged, and found herself entangled in a few brawls on my account.

It was all so confusing to me. I was being hated as a result of being associated with Arabs, even though I was not Arab. But even more confusing was why people seemed to have such an anti-Arab sentiment in the first place, when the war we were in was about rescuing and aiding the Arabs in Kuwait. I thought we were on their side. So why was I taking so much heat for being associated with their group?

Once during that time, as I walked to the post office, an older white gentleman suddenly began to charge right at me, apparently to attack me. He was shouting obscenities and looked like he was very angry at something. I did not know at what or whom, because I certainly hadn't done anything to him and didn't think I deserved that kind of treatment. I quickly got back into my car and drove off as he angrily ranted and raved, waving his fist in the air. I drove straight home. I didn't tell my parents what had happened, because they would surely become terrified and worry for my safety. I also feared that they would make me take off my hijab.

As it was, my parents were already being questioned about why they allowed me to observe the practice. Their friends wondered why a young girl who was born, raised, and educated in America would want to wear such an ugly thing. Why would I choose to do such a thing in a land of the greatest "modernity" and "freedom"? They couldn't believe that I would observe this practice that made me stick out so much rather than do what everyone else was trying to do: fit in and assimilate.

I really expected that my struggles would be centered around my interactions with non-Muslim society. But to my surprise, the most poisonous reactions came from within my own Muslim group, particularly within the Afghan community. Although these Afghans were all Muslims who were well acquainted with the underlying principles of wearing the hijab, most of them were vehemently opposed to adopting this way of life. Not only was the effort not commended, it was seen as altogether un-Afghan. In fact it was perceived as a very Arab thing to do, and emulating Arabs is seen as contradictory to upholding the Afghan identity.

I am not sure how such anti-Arab sentiment developed among Afghans, especially since many of the prophets of Islam, along with the last messenger, Muhammad (pbuh), were Arab. But this ethnocentrism is not directed against just Arabs. For example, Afghans generally view Iranians as being two-faced, with swift tongues that do not convey their true feelings. For Afghans, this is a grave weakness of character. Pakistanis are similarly conceived of as weak people who are not strong-willed or strong-hearted in the way Afghans are—my dad would say, "We used to invade their country (then part of India) just for fun." Of course these are general stereotypes among Afghans, and have nothing to do with individuals. Stereotypes are accepted because of ignorance, a problem that plagues us due to a severe lack of education. Although Islamic ideals say that there is to be brotherhood among all Muslims, this is not reflected in the real practices of Muslim countries, which certainly do not act like brothers.

Nonetheless, my aunts, uncles, and cousins—even my grandmother, who initiated my religious resurgence—were unhappy about my decision to cover my hair. They believed it would cause me to stand out in society and suffer as a result of it. Of course, my father was glad to see me dress conservatively, but unhappy that I took it to this "extreme." My grandmother told me that this was not the dress of Afghanistan, and that if I wanted to cover my hair I should do it like she did, with a thin, sheer material called *gach*, which is traditional for Afghan women. But of course, the religious requirement is for women to cover their hair, not simply shroud it with a symbolic kind of veil that really doesn't cover anything or serve any true purpose. I was completely covering my hair with thick, opaque scarves so that my hair could not be viewed by the public. When I tried to explain to her that using *gach* missed the point, she said that I was too much under the influence of Arabs and I should find room for my Afghan identity within Islam.

My critics repeated the same old lines: "When in Rome, do as the Romans do," and "As long as your heart is clean, you do not have to observe these practices." This mentality seemed like a cop-out to me, because a clean heart is something that people strive to achieve through the process of religious observation. People's hearts are not inherently predisposed to positive or negative inclinations. What does a clean heart constitute in the first place? When I asked these "clean heart" believers what they meant by this justification for forgoing religious obligations, they simply told me that if you do not lie, cheat, steal, or do other such obvious misdeeds, then you will be all right. I saw this amended version of Islam as part of a desire to modernize the religion, to adapt it to fit our needs, so that God's agenda would revolve around our own lives rather than vice versa.

On the day of my high school graduation, after three years of being looked upon as an outcast and deviant by both American and Afghan societies, I finally took off my hijab, which had caused so much contempt. I simply couldn't handle the scrutiny of my personal life. Even more ridiculous than being treated as a lesser human being because of my physical traits, I was being treated that way because of my *clothes*. And people had somehow assigned me the position of representing the entire religion of Islam. If I were to do one thing wrong or make one human mistake, I would not pay for it alone—so would Islam. If I so much as wore some lip gloss, I would be met with the attitude of "See, and she is supposed to be so religious—they're all just a bunch of hypocrites!"

I felt the pressure of trying to defend and represent a religion that not only outsiders but even its own followers criticized with so much passion. Some people tried to console me by saying that Muslims didn't like to see a young girl wearing the hijab because it reminded them of their own weaknesses or of their failure to follow the tenets of their religion. But I felt that the stigma came from their inability to understand their religion.

How is it possible for people that identify as Muslim not to understand their religion? One reason is that the Afghan languages are different from Arabic, so most Afghans can't read the Quran without some kind of translation. In Afghanistan, very few Qurans with Dari translations are available. And because much of the population is illiterate, people are doubly vulnerable to the interpretations fed to them by others. Many Afghans rely for translation on local mullahs or spiritual guides, who give them their own version of what Islam means. Often, the mullahs intermingle their own personal views with what they say Islam means. This has made it more difficult for Afghan Muslims (as well as for other Muslims who don't read Arabic) to gain a true understanding of their own religion, that is free from culture and politics. I felt that if Muslims truly understood their own religion, they wouldn't judge me for my decision to follow it in a meaningful way or ascribe to it ulterior political or cultural motives.

I was swimming against the waves, and I simply had no energy to do it anymore. I felt like the candle of my fire for God and faith had burned out. This was a tragedy in my life, because when I removed my scarf, my fellow Afghans once again judged me, telling me that I debased the institution of hijab by putting it on and taking it off and that I hurt people's perception of the religion of Islam. I was referred to for years as the girl who "used to wear hijab, and look at her now." I simply could not win. I was up against ignorant criticisms that were too unreasonable to dignify with serious responses.

Yet strangely enough, once I did remove my head covering, I felt as though people were more interested and willing to hear about Islam from me. When I wore the Muslim woman's dress, people automatically assumed that I was some sort of fundamentalist, a terrorist, or a zealot preaching the religion. When I uncovered my hair, an understanding of Islam seemed to slip into people's consciousness during our conversations; the people I met were actually impressed that someone of my age group and social standing would be so in tune to Islam. In effect it allowed me to live as a better Muslim, because I could practice my religion without any public scrutiny or expectations.

The experience of wearing the hijab was not a waste nor entirely negative, although unfortunately the negative things stand out in people's minds. I grew tremendously during that three-year-long experience, and my spirituality evolved and matured as a result of covering my hair. There were always kind people who would ask me about the principles behind wearing hijab, or Afghans who told me that I made them so proud—that I had grown up in America and yet still celebrated my faith. In fact, I received many compliments from the more God-conscious people in the Muslim and Afghan communities; but these were only a small minority in my realm of experience.

Regardless of other people's perceptions and views, my personal belief about wearing the hijab was and continues to revolve greatly around social position. The hijab is worn only outside of the home and is thus a social institution. What I absolutely loved about the hijab was how seriously I was taken in educational and professional settings. Before wearing it, my appearance and sexuality were factors in my social dealings, as they are again today now that I don't cover my hair. While wearing the hijab, I was treated as an equal counterpart whom people listened to. People paid attention to me for my opinions and what I had to say, not my physical appearance. I heard no more whistles or derogatory comments when walking in public. Most of that was replaced with hateful glares and gawking. But generally, my opinions were not taken lightly. I commanded respect when doing business, writing for the school paper, giving talks, and making guest appearances at various organizations. I was treated in a manner that was dignified and never demeaning to me as a person.

The burqa is designed to perform a similar social utility. The burqa is not an Islamic requirement; it is based on custom and is traditional to Afghanistan. Women who wear burqas take the Islamic requirements a step further in their attire. Many people view the burqa as a divider between women and the world, when in fact its oppressive qualities are not a result of the burqa itself but rather of the laws pertaining to it. Many Afghan women have vocalized their concern that the international community is placing too much emphasis upon their dress rather than getting to the heart of matters that beset their country. The veil is not seen as something that should be at the forefront of the issues. For many, it is a superficial issue, secondary to the other more central topics in question. In fact, despite their being told that they no longer have to wear the burqa, many have decided to continue to wear it until they feel reassured about the new government and its objectives. Dress should be an individual choice, as it was under the king's rule. While there will be those who are glad to be rid of it, others will continue to adopt their cultural dress nonetheless.

When I think about that stage of my life and why a simple head scarf, a small piece of fabric, would provoke so much hatred, I immediately think of the stereotypes that circulate about covered women and about the now-infamous burqa, which has become a symbol of oppression and tyranny. Among non-Muslims as well as Muslims who look down on the principles of their religion, the hijab—and the burqa even more so—is seen as an instrument that the men of the Middle East use to suppress their women. An instant connection is made between a woman covering her body and systematic oppression and submissiveness. It is true that Middle Eastern culture inflicts injustice and unfairness upon women as well as upon various other members of its society, but this is not a reflection of the religion. Many Christians and Jews who live in the same Middle Eastern countries adopt these practices without believing in Islam. It is not Islam that promotes these practices, but rather the culture and sometimes the politics of the Middle East.

More than ten years after the Gulf War, I watch my only sister, the lovely Haseena, going through some of the same struggles I went through. She is my greatest confidante. I share the innermost details of my mind, heart, and soul with her without fear of judgment, because she understands me completely. Amazingly, she has pulled me through the most difficult trials of life while I thought I, the older sister, was pulling her through. I feel that our bond is of soul and spirit rather than mere flesh and blood. Haseena's inner beauty far surpasses her outer beauty, and through her life I have grown to understand much of my own.

After the events of September 11, she encountered a great deal of stereotyping and questioning at her university as a result of her Afghan heritage. She felt that her country and religion had become demonized. When she saw that she was being viewed not as an American or even Afghan-American but quite clearly as a foreign and perhaps enemy Afghan, she began to feel pushed toward her Afghan self. And in time, Haseena started to cover her hair and wear the hijab.

Though perhaps not ready for such a bold step into her Muslim identity, she gave it her all. She engaged in religious activism both on and off campus. But she too ended up removing the hijab because of the social pressures it ignited from all sides, especially in the Afghan community. Still, the experience has changed Haseena's outlook on how she is really perceived. She does not feel as fully and unconditionally accepted as an American as she had previously. A door closed on her innocence. But another door opened for her, to an entire world that she has only begun to have the pleasure of discovering.

My younger brother Omar has dealt with Islam in a more private fashion. He is six-foot-four, a towering, tall-dark-and-handsome lad with a great head on his shoulders. He is even-tempered despite his Afghan genes, always rational, and a person of substance and character. He is a product of the same humanities magnet high school program that I attended at Grover Cleveland High School, so we have a great deal in common in how we think. But unlike me, Omar chose not to attend MSA meetings. He found them superficial. He did not associate with the religious members of the community. He eventually delved more into mainstream American college life. Even so, he has always associated himself with the ideals of his Afghan heritage, maintaining his dignity and taking the high road in all situations.

Many of the pressures that Haseena and I faced were simply

nonexistent for Omar because he is a man, and perhaps this is the reason he didn't feel the need to explore his religious identity as deeply as we did. At some point, we really felt the pressure to choose between one system or another. For even if Haseena and I didn't care what other Afghans thought about us, our reputations were connected to our parents, and they would have to live with our actions. Omar, on the other hand, was not subject to any scrutiny. Afghans never pointed their fingers at any of the men in the community for practices such as dating and drinking. Even though our parents do not have a double standard, our culture and larger society does.

Yet since September 11, Omar has deepened his awareness of his Islamic identity and especially his Afghan self. Like the rest of us, he was devastated by the war on terrorism that targeted Afghanistan. When people on radio talk shows commented on how they wanted the country to be demolished and bombed back to the Stone Age, Omar was torn: He wanted safety and security in America, yet not at the cost of the innocent Afghan people.

Omar began calling in to these talk shows, always as the voice of reason, saying, "Yes, I am an Afghan-American man, and I don't mind waiting at the airport for an extra half-hour if they have to run a security check on me because of my name or racial group, as long as they can prevent future attacks on America." But when people said they would like to see Afghanistan destroyed, he couldn't stomach it. He would come to me in frustration saying, "I can't believe how ignorant people are in our society. Why can't they get it through their heads that the Afghans are not the ones who attacked on September 11?" I tried to console him. I was used to the blatant attacks on Afghans and Muslims. My brother had somehow been sheltered from them, perhaps as a result of his lack of involvement in the Muslim community.

Omar suddenly started finding more meaningful things to do on Friday and Saturday evenings than going out with his friends. He stayed at home to follow the news. He was drawn in by shows that invited Muslim guests, his favorite being *Hardball with Chris Matthews*. He would call me up at all hours of the night saying, "Why do they always pick these airhead Muslims to represent us on TV?"

"So why don't you speak up, then?" I asked him.

Speaking up was something he had always shied away from. However, he finally took the initiative to start an organization with my sister and me, the Afghan Institute of Development, that focuses on correcting misconceptions and widening awareness about Afghans and Muslims, as well as helping our community here and in Afghanistan. He is also becoming more involved in politics, and hopes to contribute an Afghan-American voice to American political life. The events of September 11 have raised Omar's consciousness of how he is seen in our society and that he must live with that perception of his identity whether he chooses to or not.

I realize that my own struggle to "find myself" in between cultural identities is natural to any assimilation process that pioneering generations face, regardless of the country they migrate from. I have since been able to place my experiences in perspective and alleviate much of the confusion I faced in marrying my Afghan and my American self.

When I first attempted to meld these two identities in my own life, I had no model for the synthesis. I was among the very first Afghans to be born in the U.S., so I had to create that identity on my own. The process of self-discovery opened my eyes to a sea of knowledge about myself and my culture, as well as the cultures of others. It was through my unique set of experiences, which included community involvement and activism, that I was given opportunities to grow into the person I have become.

I found community activism an effective way to dispel myths about and shed light upon my religion. I felt the task was twofold, because both the Muslim and non-Muslim communities needed education about Islam as it existed outside of the corrupt practices of its followers and the politics of the Middle East. I used conferences, television programs, school-based organizations, and every available forum to clarify the truth about Islam and its distinction from Middle Eastern culture. Doing so allowed me to gain the confidence and strength to overcome feelings of shame, animosity, and self-hatred. Such feelings are common among Muslims. Scores of Iranians I've met have converted from Islam to other religions as a result of the actions of the Ayatollah Khomeini and his regime.

I have learned and now realize that everyone in society, and I in particular, need to become active in the community. We start by figuring out what we are personally invested in, intellectually and emotionally. We all hold certain issues close to our hearts. It seems criminal to me to remain apathetic when we have the opportunity and ability to do our part to improve circumstances. We don't have to become radical, but we should use what we do best to help a cause that we believe in wholeheartedly. Usually my efforts are fruitful, but sometimes they yield no results. In any case, I can rest assured that I have done my part and made my contribution to a society that has given me much.

By educating others, I myself was able to gain a deeper understanding of Islam that was truer to its essence and free from the hype surrounding it. I began to realize why I had to struggle so hard when I was wearing the hijab. It was not the spiritual aspect or the modesty of the hijab that people objected to, but the violent image of the Arabs and the mystical portrayal of Islam that was so uncomfortable for them. It was an image that nobody wanted to be confronted with, and so I was loathed for a scarf that I wore over my hair. Now I understood why.

In my experience, I find more practical implementations of Islamic principles in the West than in many "Islamic" countries. For instance, the amount of money that is poured into welfare, aid, and humanitarian organizations is quite significant here. If you happen to have a disability or to belong to an underprivileged class of people, there are many programs to help level the playing field. If you have a problem with domestic violence or other kinds of abuse, our society offers many avenues that people can take advantage of so they don't have to resort to desperate measures. Even animals are shown extraordinary concern and are treated with the utmost dignity and respect. These are all principles that are deeply embedded in Islamic conduct. However, looking at the current state of Muslim countries around the globe, one does not generally find such practices. Many Islamic principles have become what I like to call "dead knowledge," or knowledge that is not acted upon. The Islamic countries are well aware of their duties and responsibilities to their people, yet they do not act upon them. If the leaders of these countries carried out and justly adhered to their obligations, then why would so many people flee from them to the West?

Interestingly, if I had lived in Afghanistan during its more open years and decided to wear the Islamic head covering in Kabul as opposed to the *gach* scarves, I would most likely be reprimanded with the Afghan version of the expression "When in Rome, do as the Romans do." Social conformity was key there, and I would most likely be frowned upon for undertaking such a practice, even though in a Muslim country. In America I am free to wear a veil, cover my hair, and practice any other beliefs as long as they don't harm anyone else or myself. Although many Americans, most of whom are not Muslim, may not always welcome it, and while many frown upon the veil as a symbol of oppression, I still have the right to dress as I please in this country.

In 2002, only months after the attacks on America, I watched an Oprah Winfrey program called "Why I Came to America." The program explored the personal experiences of immigrants from a colorful spectrum of backgrounds ranging from East to West, from South America to Ireland, from Vietnam to Afghanistan. Although the specifics of each person's experiences and reasons for leaving their birthplaces varied, their reasons for coming to

America were all the same. They desired freedom, liberty, and opportunity. These were the simple ingredients that their own countries lacked but that America offered. In the exodus out of Afghanistan and into America and the West, one finds countless stories as to why Afghans left behind their homes, jobs, and life savings. It is a huge risk when a family decides to pick up all they have and leave one country for a life in another country, with no certainty of their future. America offers people throughout the world a second chance at life when they see no other hope for change or success.

With the latest developments in Afghanistan, many Afghans might want to return to their original birthplace; others will call America their real home and will want to remain here indefinitely. My own family definitely hopes to go back to Afghanistan to offer our support and give back some of what we have gained here. This would probably translate into a three- or four-year commitment to work in the country. As for moving there permanently, I suppose it would depend on how we feel living in a land that has become foreign through its years of transformation, as well as our own years of transformation abroad; how well we are received, because we might be perceived as outsiders; what kinds of relationships and bonds we build; and whether it will even be allowed. I am very interested to see what is in store for the Afghan-Americans who go back to Afghanistan, now that it has gone from a thriving state to a failed state to a recovering state. Many Afghans, including my parents, hope that it will reassemble itself into the Afghanistan that they left under the rule of the king. But inevitably those fond memories of their country under the rule of the royal family will remain in the past. What emerges from the current state of affairs will be a new and different Afghanistan.

~⚬ *Five* ⚬~

Revisiting Afghanistan

Without truly realizing what was happening or why, as I grew up in America, I watched the happy and beautiful Afghanistan that I knew from memories and from the stories of my parents endure such trauma that I could hardly recognize it anymore. The lovely bazaars, the engaging people, the gorgeous landscape and awe-inspiring works of architecture were nowhere to be found in the media coverage I saw and the eyewitness accounts I heard. People were fear-stricken, hardened, and dying without any meaning or justification.

After years of this kind of portrayal of the beautiful country I had long ago visited, I myself began to hate its failures. I began to resent that Afghans couldn't get their country together or get with the political program. I hated the fact that they allowed themselves to fall prey to foreign invasions, that they couldn't feed their own people. If these were truly intelligent, compassionate, and capable people, as my parents kept trying to convince me when they wanted me to be proud of my heritage, then why were they constantly being used and abused by foreign powers? I saw how Afghans always blamed their neighbors for interfering in the internal affairs of the country. But why did they fall prey to the Soviets, the British, or even the Pakistanis in the first place? If they had a handle on their country to begin with, how could any foreign influence gain a foothold? I turned to my parents and their friends, in fact to anyone who was acquainted enough with the country and had some semblance of reason, for answers about why this had happened to Afghanistan.

The best Afghan government that most Afghans remember was the monarchy of Zahir Shah, who ruled from 1933 to 1973. He was known for being just and merciful. He had an ingenious way of bringing people together, downplaying their differences and encouraging the various ethnic groups to intermarry. By doing so, he won the respect of most Afghans, even of underrepresented minorities.

Aslam Aseel, a member of the king's royal guard, recalls many instances of his employer's merciful temperament. Aseel guarded him for more than two decades, and says that during that time no attempts were made on the life of his noble king. He never noticed any real threats to Zahir Shah nor felt hostility toward himself. Aseel remarks on the king's strong distaste for violence and bloodshed. He did not condone capital punishment, even for those convicted of the worst crimes. Though he ultimately allowed family members of a victim to decide the fate of the convicted, he worked to sway them toward mercy by meeting with them, trying to persuade them that execution would not bring back their loved one and that they should forgive the loss. Aseel says that if the victim's family refused to be lenient, the king usually left town during the execution, as he truly hated the taking of human life.

The people of Afghanistan grew to adore Zahir Shah to the extent that they referred to him as God's shadow, *Sayah Khudawand*. Today, an 86-year-old Aslam Aseel says that he swore his loyalty to the king when he entered his service and will die with that loyalty engraved on his heart. He says that he would not give his loyalty blindly to any human being, but that Zahir Shah truly gained his trust, loyalty, and respect over many years. Their close working relationship developed into undying reverence.

In 1964, Zahir Shah called for the drafting of a new constitution. This constitution was to be drawn up by a *loya jirga*, a grand assembly composed of both appointees and of people elected in provinces across the country. This assembly represented all ethnic groups and balanced the spectrum of opinions held by the diverse population. In fact, loya jirgas had been called by leaders of Afghanistan since the 1700s and had become more common since World War I. They were called on an as-needed basis to handle issues immediately affecting the country, ensuring that they were properly and fairly attended to. Under Zahir Shah, a *shura*, or parliament, was also in place to provide leadership on day-to-day affairs. The shura included representatives of all ethnic groups and was intent on fairly representing their interests.

The 1964 constitution had several progressive provisions. It replaced the absolute monarchy with a constitutional one and prohibited the royal family (other than the king) from participating in government. It strengthened individual rights and loosened certain religious mandates. It provided for an independent judiciary and a bicameral legislature. In 1965, national elections were held and the constitution went into effect.

When I was first learning about Afghanistan, it was hard for me to believe that this level of progressiveness could be instituted under a monarchy. Growing up in a society where elected government is essential to our way of life, I had to rethink how I judged the value of different kinds of governments. My parents had a great deal of reverence for King Zahir Shah. There did seem to be something noble and elegant about a king—a feeling that I did not get from elected presidents in the United States. The king of Afghanistan was almost worshipped, treated benevolently, and respected; the presidents I saw were ridiculed and belittled. Though I agreed with having an elected government, I was intrigued with the loyalty, admiration, and devotion that people showed their kings.

My mother says that when Afghan students protested against Zahir Shah, her father had told her that they were taking him for granted and would one day wish they had him back. More than thirty years later, that prediction seems to have come true. Under Zahir Shah, the country was at peace. Afghans were relatively better off than those who came before or after them. But there was also discontent. Some people felt that the king could do more to stimulate economic growth. Some freedoms were still withheld. The country still lacked technological conveniences that other nations enjoyed.

Ironically, when Afghanistan's government set out on the path to economic growth, freedom, and modernization in the 1960s, it made itself more vulnerable to discontent. For example, during Zahir Shah's reign, Islam was not forcefully imposed upon the Afghan people. Afghans also enjoyed certain freedoms of expression and speech. But this attempt to tolerate varying opinions, even those contrary to the government's, allowed a small minority of Communists to gain a foothold within the system. Among the students who had used their freedom to criticize the Afghan government were those who would eventually overthrow that government, force their ideology upon the population, and open the door to the Soviets.

In the U.S., freedom of speech is one of our most cherished rights. In theory we are willing to tolerate dissent, even the most ferocious criticism, in the name of upholding this essential freedom. Of course, freedom of expression will not necessarily foster such disastrous consequences as occurred in Afghanistan. But there were holes in the Afghan system that made such freedom a bigger threat than it is in America. A parallel example might be found in the September 11 attacks. Some Americans have said that our high degree of freedom allowed the attacks to happen, because it let the terrorists organize and make plans while hiding from our intelligence agencies under the shield of civil liberties. But the purpose of those terrorists was to make a violent statement against America's foreign policy. The targets they chose were highly symbolic. They were not seriously trying to oust President

Bush and take over America's government. To do so would certainly seem impossible. It was not so impossible in Afghanistan. There, the line between freedom and the sanctity of government was far thinner.

Under Zahir Shah's reign, Afghan women enjoyed a great deal of freedom relative to previous times. They composed almost half of the workforce. They were able to drive and enjoy other freedoms that were once reserved for men. Women dominated the education arena. Most teachers were women, and they were responsible for teaching sixteen subjects to their students.

Women were not entirely free in the Western sense; the conservative society held women in a designated place. For example, it was not until the Communist government came into power that women were allowed to enter the entertainment industry without fear of social persecution. Entertainment flourished with a new crop of female Afghan entertainers. It was also under Communism that they were able to go to nightclubs and drink freely. Women drinking and dancing in this fashion had been unheard of and unacceptable before. But modernization did not automatically bring freedom. Many liberties promised by the Communists never materialized, and others were rigidly curtailed. Conformity was key, and people could not swim against the tide as they had been able to under Zahir Shah.

Before the Soviet invasion, Afghanistan was a poor country, but it did not seem to have a big problem with homelessness or other problems to be expected in economically weak areas. One would imagine that the streets of such a poor country would be filled with beggars looking for scraps; or in the case of the homeless, looking for a warm, quiet place to take shelter for the night. Several factors in Afghan society helped alleviate this problem. Housing was quite cheap, and Afghans usually acquired homes through inheritance. Also, family ties were very strong, so those threatened with homelessness could appeal to a relative who would be likely to take them in.

There were also government-sponsored locations for the home-less, *maraatoon* (beggar's house), in which people could take shel-ter permanently. These shelters generally were occupied by handicapped, mentally disabled, or otherwise dysfunctional peo-ple who for a variety of reasons could not help themselves to attain the necessities of life. In addition to this form of welfare, Afghans could apply to the Red Crescent organization for temporary fi-nancial relief. Qualified recipients would receive cash, food, and clothing. People used the options they had to avoid becoming homeless. This did not mean that their housing was luxurious by any standard—much of it would be considered substandard by contemporary conceptions—but it served its purpose.

Finally, Afghans considered it taboo to fall into such a state of helplessness, and worked very hard to make sure that it didn't happen. The only time they would be seen begging or homeless was when there was no alternative. Certainly, being homeless car-ries negative connotations in cultures throughout the world, and no one tries to become homeless on purpose. But other-directed-ness is key to survival in the Afghan community, and one's reputa-tion (which is based on the strength of one's principles rather than financial status) significantly alters the fabric of one's life. How a family is seen in the eyes of other Afghans is of monumental im-portance. The treatment that one received in school, the opportu-nities that were available in the workforce, and the distribution of goods in society relied heavily upon one's place within the social hierarchy.

Despite the various social nets, many Afghans lived in poverty. Meanwhile, the royal family naturally lived in wealth and luxury. Some believed that the royal family was too consumed with fulfill-ing its own needs and desires to be able to sincerely heed the needs of the people. Communism, on the other hand, promised that everyone would be guaranteed at least a minimum lifestyle that would include the essentials of food, clothing, and shelter—*dodai, kalai,* and *kour* in Pashto. Communists also promised land ownership to Afghans. That was a great promise for those who struggled hard for very little in return and were desperate for hope. Of course, the promise never materialized under Communist rule. A friend of mine recalls a man who publicly asked, "They promised us food, clothing, and shelter. Well, where is it? I have yet to see any food, clothing, or shelter!" The man was taken away and executed for daring to pose such a defiant question. The Communists openly declared their intention to destroy those who stood in their way—they were more than willing to fulfill *that* promise.

In Afghanistan, as in every society, the wealthy and affluent lived a life of privilege, and being in the lowest position promised undesirable ways of life. Success also clearly depended on whom one knew rather than what one knew. Though not outwardly stated, it was apparent that those in positions of authority were closely tied to one another through lineage, such as the Mohammadzais (the agreed-upon "top lineage" to which the royal family belonged) or those closely associated with them. But to be in the right circles and gain the exposure necessary to attain those connections, they had to develop personalities and etiquette that befitted the social codes.

One Afghan gentleman I met, Jamal, who had lived in the province of Qunduz, surprised me when he told me that he would not want to go back to Afghanistan even if it were completely freed. Usually, Afghans I meet who left the country after age thirty show a desperate longing to return to their birthplace. I was so used to hearing the broken record of homesickness that Jamal really astounded me. His reason was that upward mobility in Afghanistan was only possible for a specific, privileged class that was tightly knit and impossible to break into.

Jamal describes himself as one of the majority of Afghans who did not live in Kabul, whose parents were not literate or well-connected and had no property or desirable alliances. If he hadn't taught himself to read and write, Jamal says, he too would be illiterate. He cringed at the lack of opportunity for rural Afghans:

"We were the best and the brightest of Afghanistan, but we were never given a chance. When some of our exceptional countrymen from the rural provinces managed to go to Kabul University, they proved themselves to be the most successful and talented students, whom the other Kabuli students envied and admired."

Jamal says that he felt that the people of Kabul looked down upon him and those in the rural suburbs. So after coming to America and finding a wealth of opportunities available to him and his family, he says that for the first time in generations, they are in control of their livelihood and have a real possibility of upward mobility. He asks, "Why would I give all of this up and take my family back to its helplessness?" I replied that economic conditions should improve in all areas of Afghanistan, but my words fell on deaf ears. Jamal said that it would be many years before Afghans of the rural provinces had the same privileges and opportunities as the people of Kabul. Until then, he said, "I will stay in America, where I am treated with the dignity that allows me the same opportunities as any other—even the same as the son of the president!"

While my parents and their friends do not share exactly the same perspective as Jamal, they agree that the country's downfall was largely because of a failure to strategically employ its human resources, particularly during the 1960s and early 1970s, when they were going to college and maturing into young adults. As they saw it, all of the wrong people were given all of the right positions. The leaders of the country, from governors, mayors, and ministers all the way up the political hierarchy, were generally unfit for their jobs. Many lacked the necessary training and character for their positions. Some were selfish individuals who attained their titles through connections or social position, and did not see their posts as opportunities to serve the people but to serve themselves and those to whom they wanted to extend their privileges. In the post-Taliban government led by President Hamid Karzai, the same issue continues to haunt the country: employing human resources based on qualification rather than ethnicity, political affiliation, or social connections.

Not everyone in Afghanistan had equal access to education. Afghans like Jamal who were living in underdeveloped areas did not enjoy the same social privileges or access to resources that would allow them to gain the skills necessary to succeed academically. People living in rural areas earned most of their income from agricultural use of their land. This required a great deal of labor, which forced children into work at early ages. Thus generations of illiterate people had no prospect of breaking out of their socioeconomic class. If a child's parents and grandparents had known only a life of hard labor and did not even introduce their children to the notion of education and advancement, how could children be expected to do so on their own? And if they had to spend their days in the fields rather than in school, they certainly would have no chance to gain the skills needed to access the channels of financial success.

One usually regards the educational arena as a place that cultivates and fosters growth and helps to actualize peoples' talents and interests, directing them into the appropriate fields of work and study. This system of education on the whole is intended to help people succeed in whatever they are good at, regardless of whether it is in the hard sciences, behavioral sciences, or arts and humanities. Unfortunately, this commonsense system was not implemented in Afghanistan. My parents themselves were products of such university selection processes. A person who was good at mathematics but who scored higher in another section of the Concorde exam was placed in the area of their highest score. In essence, this college entrance exam decided not only whether the candidate would be admitted to the university, but also which department they would be admitted to. Students had no real say in the department of their choice, as their test scores sealed their educational fate.

You could not intentionally score poorly in the areas you were not interested in because you could not get into the university at all if you got a low overall score on the test. Therefore, you were compelled to do the very best you could possibly do to ensure that you would at least gain acceptance to a university, with no thought as to the secondary issue of the particular department you wanted. Students were happy just to be accepted in the competitive environment for admission into the only university, Kabul University. The exception was the medical students who lived in rural areas and were not planning on coming to Kabul to pursue medical studies. These students applied directly to the only other higher education institute in Afghanistan, the Medical School of Jalalabad/Nangarhar.

Were Afghan regimes afraid that they would lose control over the country if its people were to become comfortable and rich? A relative of mine recalls the time that an Afghan head of state brought a group of statesmen to a barn. In this barn were many starving chickens. The minute this official began feeding the chickens, they flocked to his side. But when the chickens were full, they simply walked away. The moral of the story was that people who were in need would need their ruler, while satisfied and comfortable people would not. Though this insecurity on the part of those in power seems absurd and gravely immoral, nonetheless it happened time and time again in a variety of forms in Afghanistan.

In the early part of the 1970s, as Afghanistan began to blossom, many of its people felt that the country should be built up in all facets and should catch up to the standard of living of the rest of the modern world. The Afghan people saw themselves as bright, intelligent, and hardworking, and there was no reason why they should be lagging behind. My parents and their peers lament that this attitude led to too much admiration for outsiders and not enough for their own people and country. Key politicians were more interested in the ways of other countries and their people than their own (this admiration of others is referred to as *palah been*). They were dazzled by those countries' wealth, power, and prestige. Their mentality allowed them to fall victim to the outsiders' webs of self-interest and desire to dominate.

When Daoud Khan toppled the king in 1973, he claimed to be setting up a "democratic" government in which he was the self-proclaimed new president. He sympathized and allied himself with Communist ideologies that preached the need for a minimal standard of life for all, and kept close ties with Communists.[1] He believed in a stronger, modern Afghanistan that would be able to compete in the world economy. Indeed, he was a visionary who began to implement a revolutionary five-year plan that brought innovative technology such as television to the country for the first time, and who foresaw a bright and economically fit future.

Education was a huge part of modernization efforts. Professors who taught at Kabul University recall that prior to the invasion, the Soviet government offered many scholarships for Afghan students to study in the Soviet Union. Naturally, the opportunity to study abroad is an appealing offer for students in any part of the world. Universities in Afghanistan were scarce, very prestigious, and extremely hard to gain admission to. Competition was rigorous. Those who did not get accepted to a university would learn a technical skill and work in that field. Students who received Soviet scholarships were the cream of the crop and could most certainly get into Kabul University anyway, but usually opted to take the scholarships to study abroad and improve their chances at loftier goals.

When these students began their studies in the Soviet Union, they were usually tacitly persuaded to adopt Communist ways and to incorporate them into Afghan ways. No contradiction or conflict was seen between the two ways of living. The Afghan and Communist ways were promoted as compatible, in fact as a strong and cohesive synthesis that would prove beneficial to the people

---

[1] Abdul Samad Ghaus. *The Fall of Afghanistan: An Insider's Account.* Pergamon-Brassey's International Defense Publishers, 1988.

of Afghanistan, and perhaps even deliver them from their lack of progress.

These new Afghan Communists formed a loyalty to what they called their "Mother Russia." Russia was not necessarily glorified as a nation, so such loyalty did not clash with their Afghan nationalistic pride. Rather, Russia was seen as a kind of utopia that promised heaven on earth for downtrodden Afghans. The professed intention of the Communist Afghans was not to sell out their country but to help pull it out of its stagnant state. These Communists did not see themselves as being anti-Afghanistan; rather, they thought that they were the most loyal to the country, since they were struggling to revolutionize it. When these "enlightened" students returned home, they began to organize. Under Zahir Shah, they expressed their new ideas, demonstrated against the government, and even openly criticized Islam.

Some elder Afghans feared that allowing more education would lead to a loss of God-consciousness among the youth—God-consciousness being all of the morals and values expected to be upheld by those who have the faith of God in their hearts. In Afghanistan, Islam was the form of God-consciousness that the vast majority of people practiced. These elders' concerns were largely dismissed as being old-fashioned and closed-minded. But many Afghan Communists really did want to rid Afghanistan of its strong faith in Islam. They believed Islamic values held the country down—not because of Islam's particular precepts, but because they believed that religion of any kind was incompatible with progress and material success.

Throughout the years, I have come across many of these products of the Russian education system. One element they all have in common is that they adamantly profess not to be Communists even as they defend Communism's doctrines. A gentleman I know named Hafizullah got his PhD in the former Soviet Union. He is an intelligent fellow who frankly blames the Afghans for not being able to understand properly the true ideals of Communism. He says that while he himself is not a Communist, he had to pose as one during Afghanistan's Communist regime in order to survive, as did many others who concealed their personal views in favor of self-preservation. Still, he says, Afghans never gave the Communists a chance to fully implement their plans for change, but ignorantly attacked them out of hand. Hafizullah says that Afghans were too shallow and narrow-minded to be able to grasp the change that Communism offered because of a lack of education and of access to the world outside of Afghanistan. He claims that if they had given it a chance and followed its course correctly, it would have benefited the Afghans tremendously.

Hafizullah admits that his peers began to organize when they returned to Afghanistan from Russia, and that they had certainly hoped that the country would open itself to the light of Communism. Still, he insists that Communism did not necessarily have to undercut Islam, since religion could remain in the mosques where it belonged—there could be a separation of church and state. Islam could be maintained, but Communism could answer the prayers of the Afghans who wanted progress and a bright future for their country.

I asked Hafizullah the obvious question: "Why do you think Communism could do anything for Afghanistan when it didn't in Russia?" Surely, since it was created in Russia, Russians must have known best how to properly understand and implement it, yet it was a disaster. Hafizullah simply replied that it was not accurately carried out in Russia either, and that these ideals were too sophisticated for the simple people whom it attempted to save.

Soviet doctrine did not include the concept of God. It was a dangerous clash between ideologies. This is not to imply that if the Soviets had incorporated religion into their belief system, even Islam, it would justify an invasion or takeover. Afghanistan is and continues to be a sovereign state that demands autonomy; Pakistan would be no more welcome an invader than Russia. But the Afghan sense of God-consciousness clashed directly with Communist rules. Almost immediately after their takeover, the Communists targeted Islam in an attempt to cleanse the country of its religious belief system. For Afghans, it was this particular offense of the Communists that most justified and sparked the rising up against them. A few were able to marry their faith with Communist ideals, but most people who analyzed the situation from a basic level drew the simple conclusion that atheism and Islam do not mix.

The people of Afghanistan as a whole did not favor Communism. This is made painfully clear by the fact that so many Afghans actively resisted it to the death. By inviting Soviet forces into the country, the Afghan Communists caused their own people to suffer the loss of one and a half million lives in a hideously brutal fashion.

❧ ❧

Although history can provide us with certain answers, sometimes it's the questions that are most important. During my college years, when I began to come to terms with the real meaning of what it is to be Afghan, I finally stopped looking at Afghanistan's history for answers as to why it had failed, because I no longer needed an explanation about why my Afghan self had failed. I realized that my parents no longer needed to defend themselves or their country's failures—because we hadn't failed at all. Just as the ideals of Islam were being abused or ignored by the people who claimed to be a part of it, the true principles of being an Afghan had been neglected and abandoned. This was precisely why they were failing so miserably: because they had departed from their *true* Afghan, Muslim selves.

The Afghans in Afghanistan couldn't get back on their feet because the people who eventually gained control became corrupted and behaved in an entirely un-Afghan way. Likewise, many of the Afghans I knew here did not have the genuine qualities of a truly Afghan character: they had become savvy, slick, and shallow.

Where were these idealized people I had heard so much about? People with such high principles, people who stood by a strong code of conduct, ethical people you would want to know? I had to believe that such people still existed, but they were now scattered among the exodus of refugees. Later in life I would have the honor of meeting some of the real, or *aseel*, Afghans who never changed because of wealth, poverty, schooling, or any other kind of external force. For now, I would try to personify those ideals without looking to an individual model. I would create the model within myself.

Author dressed by her parents in traditional Afghani dress.

Author's paternal family in Kabul, Afghanistan.

Author's mother, Shaesta, during college in Paghman, Afghanistan.

Author's father, Abdul Qadeer, during college at Kabul University.

Author's parents' wedding ceremony.

Author's grandparents, Mr. and Mrs. Kamrany, on their last trip to America for their daughter Shaesta's wedding. To Shaesta's left is her elder brother, Nake Kamrany.

Author's paternal grand-
mother, Koh Koh Jan.

Author's father, Qadeer, with author's youngest
uncle, Shair (who passed away in July 2002).

Author's brother, Omar (top) with their father, Abdul Qadeer.

Author's sister, Haseena, on her baccalaureate graduation.

Author wearing a traditional Afghani dress during the wedding ceremony with her husband, Samir Aseel, on their wedding day, May 24, 1997.

During the wedding ceremony the bride and groom are covered with a Banarasi shawl to look at each other in a beautiful ornate mirror that no one has ever looked in before.

Author and her husband at their wedding reception. The palms of their hands are stained with henna according to Afghani wedding tradition.

Presidential Palace in Kabul, Afghanistan.

Paghman, Afghanistan.

⟡ Six ⟡

Womanhood

As I began to reconcile the various conflicting facets of my identity, I became a young adult with a wealth of rich experiences that were uncommon for others my age. I learned much about being a woman by emulating my mother, Shaesta, who to me is an example of a real Afghan woman.

I was told and continue to be told about my mom's beauty and popularity in her younger years. Her bold, striking features were complemented by her cutting-edge sense of style. She always stayed one step ahead of her peers by subscribing to magazines that featured the latest looks. Listening to people talk about her, I get a picture of one of those trend-setting girls we've all known in school who are mimicked by the others. But this was not how her beauty was defined; rather, it was only an added feature to her beautiful personhood.

My mom is very sharp, always thinking on her feet in situations that demand it. Her ability to get us out of Afghanistan in 1978 without having to be smuggled through the mountains is one example. My dad always let her do the talking when we needed to take care of certain business situations.

Though my mother is not from a typical Afghan socioeconomic background, she is a typical Afghan woman in the sense that she is strong-willed and devoted to her family, without compromise.

Her priorities and goals have always revolved around her family, as she derives her strength and motivation from her need to build up her children's lives. This is quite typical of Afghan women, as they do not perceive themselves as the first priority in life, but rather their children and family. They do not resent this or feel it as oppression, but as a kind of selfless and unconditional love that is real, strong, and genuine. There is no question or measurement of who did what for whom or how much—just pure love in the true sense of the word. And in this process, women such as my mother find themselves feeling increasingly beautiful and mature as their children flourish into great individuals, rather than feeling ugly or old with time.

My mom was more lenient with me than my dad. She believed that when one parent was strict, the other should provide an outlet for the children so that they would not end up hating their family, home atmosphere, or life in general. Her mellow personality blended well with my dad's much more forceful one. The synthesis of my parents' styles of raising children turned out to be a successful mix. My siblings and I were all born in the United States, but we never took our culture or religion for granted, and we have all tried to discover our roots and internalize our religious and cultural identities.

My mother had the opportunity to live in Kabul during the most modern era that existed in Afghanistan, the 1960s and '70s. It was a time of great liberation for women, when nearly all arenas of Afghan life were open to them. They were educated at the university with their male counterparts. They dressed as they saw fit. They occupied prestigious positions in all facets of society as professors, doctors, government ministers, and bankers. They reached the rank of colonel in police departments. They were permitted to enter the army. Women occupied two ministry positions and held seats as members of the parliament, or *shura-e-meli*. My mother worked for the United Nations in Kabul, and was privileged to have a driver bring her to and from work.

The historical role of Afghan women has been more complex than it is often made out to be. When Afghanistan was first being attacked by colonial powers in the 1800s, women fought side by side with men and participated in battle in all ways that were possible for them. They risked their lives to attend the injured, fed the soldiers, and performed brave deeds. Two schools in Afghanistan have been named after Malalai and Zarghuna, women renowned for their contributions to the Afghan resistance during the British invasion.

Ghaiyrat, the system of Afghan pride, holds women *(nang namoos)* in high esteem. Contrary to the usual portrayal of Eastern women, the Afghan code places a great deal of trust in women. Afghan men often store their family's wealth by investing in gold and simply having their wives wear their life savings. Because Afghanistan's governments often switched hands, banks seemed unreliable, but it was commonly accepted that women would never be touched in times of turmoil.

It is a matter of deep social confidence that women should not be harmed or shamed despite conflicts that might occur. There is an expression in Farsi that begins as follows: "You should sacrifice any and all of the wealth in the world necessary to keep yourself well and alive" *(mal fidayi sar)*. The expression continues that you should sacrifice yourself to keep your wife alive *(sar fidayi namoos)*. These expressions convey a hierarchy of priorities in life: if you lose all of your wealth and possessions, it is no matter, since your life and health are more valuable than all of the wealth in the world. Similarly, if you sacrifice yourself for your *namoos*, which literally refers to a wife but could include a mother, sister, daughter, or country, then it is no matter, since a man should rightfully be at the disposal of these entities, who are of far greater value and well worth the sacrifice.

Yet there is an alternate perception found in the West that Eastern women—and Afghan women in particular—have been suffering in silence for centuries under their brutal male masters.

Attention to the policies of the Taliban has fueled this belief, but even after the Taliban's expulsion from Afghanistan this idea persists. Women in countries such as Saudi Arabia who walk several steps behind their husbands are used as examples of general Eastern and Islamic practice, even though it is actually a specific cultural practice and certainly *not* an Islamic religious practice.

The fact that women pray behind men in the mosques is also seen as a kind of inferior treatment of women. However, Muslim prayer requires kneeling, prostration, and awkward positions, and women would not necessarily be comfortable doing such things in plain view of a congregation of men. Another reason for separating women and men during prayer is so that everyone remains sharply focused on their spiritual connection. Some mosque structures place men in front and women in back, whereas others place them on separate floors of the mosque so that the women overlook the men. But the essence is that the sexes are separated so that they can concentrate on their worship.

The fact that women are covered leads many to believe that they are somehow being hidden from society in an attempt to erase women from the public or make them as invisible as possible. Islamic dress for women does command modesty, and the purpose of modesty is to shift attention from physical appearance to who a person is as an individual. In fact, women I've encountered who follow Muslim dress feel that Western fashion for women clearly indicates that these women are simply fulfilling the desires or fantasies of men. How they dress, speak, behave, and interact in society as well as their likes and dislikes seem to be centered around the male appetite. They find the way Western women conduct themselves to be entirely subservient to and dominated by men. In sum, it seems both perspectives are extreme and highly critical of each other.

Despite these notions, many women in Afghanistan were quite liberal and lived lives that are a far cry from those who grew up after the Soviet invasion. Many privileged women in pre-Soviet

Kabul chose not to marry, a significant break from past generations. It was a boon to women that they had a real choice. But that choice represented many things: educational growth, financial independence, career opportunities, greater mobility, and so forth. In other words, the freedom that these Kabuli women found reflected myriad aspects of their lives, and not some kind of escape from domination by a husband.

It seems to me that the image of women in the East has been highly distorted: They are often portrayed as weak, timid, or wholly victimized by their male counterparts. Yet Afghan women, even under the harsh rule of the Taliban, have accomplished a great deal. They have been able to keep some semblance of schooling and health care going despite tremendous odds and in the face of physical harm. They have managed to document many of the injustices that have occurred in their country at great price. These are not the actions of weak, timid victims. Afghan women have historically upheld their value systems and have risen above the odds during times of trial and adversity.

The ill-mannered practices of "Islamic governments" perpetuate stereotypes about Muslims across the board. These governments do not accurately reflect the religion of Islam. They tend to be led by corrupt and oppressive leaders who terrorize their people into submission, using the people's blind faith as a tool. Most Muslims who live in Eastern countries do not have access to literature or religious teachers who disperse accurate information. Instead, the *mullahs*, or spiritual leaders, are often hypocritical and lacking in even basic knowledge of the principles of Islam. They have taught people to read the Quran in Arabic without translating the meaning behind the verses. Instead, the Quran has been treated as an idol, kissed and wrapped in beautiful silks and layers of other expensive fabrics, while not explored for its meaning. A sick person might rub the Quran around his or her face and chest, using it as a healing source. The Quran serves a holy and transcendental purpose rather than being strictly a practical means of teaching people how to conduct their lives.

In pre-Islamic Arabia, the pagan Arabs treated women abhorrently. Women were lowly commodities who did not even measure up to the value placed on sheep and cattle. However, the spread of the religion of Islam abolished these practices and brought the Arabs from their darkness into light. Islam and the Middle Eastern culture broke away from each other. Elements of the Eastern culture trickled back into the practices of Muslims, though, as they tried to create a synthesis between their culture and religion. Of course, Muslims are permitted to practice and celebrate their cultural customs and traditions, but only to the extent that they do not conflict with their religion. And it seems the culture of the East does clash with Islam on many fronts that have become readily apparent in this century.

People often forget that there is a huge population of Muslims who are not of Arab or Middle Eastern descent. In fact, Indonesians are the largest ethnic group among the Muslims. There are also many Muslims in Europe, such as the Bosnians and Chechnyans, as well as Muslims here in the United States. These Muslims do not fit the typical "dark" or Eastern image that we are accustomed to. They practice their own social and cultural customs and speak Western languages. There is no contradiction: Islam is a way of life that transcends all geographical boundaries.

Pre-Islamic Arab men could marry many women with no accountability to any of them. Islam held these men accountable for their wives, and restricted the number of wives a man could have to four. This notion of polygamy presents a huge barrier to understanding for people unfamiliar with Islam. Muslims do not view polygamy as a backward practice. They *do* think that enjoying women in relationships other than socially recognizable marriage is entirely backward. The institutions of dating and living with a domestic partner, or bearing children with a person who does not own up to the responsibilities and accountability that a marriage dictates, is seen as quite shallow and base. Adultery is also totally shunned, as it leads to so many social plagues that debase the trust and foundation of family institutions. Muslims view such treatment of women as abusive, demeaning, and extremely oppressive toward women.

Muslims believe that by legalizing polygamy, a limit is set on the number of relationships possible in a lifetime. Thus, the relationships must be treated quite seriously, requiring a great deal of responsibility and accountability in financial and social commitments. For instance, as opposed to a girlfriend, a wife has the right to take her husband's name if she so chooses, as do her children. She and her offspring enjoy inheritance rights in the event that her husband passes away. She is socially recognized as the legal wife of the man with whom she lives and bears children. From a Muslim perspective, this is a more dignified way to live than being technically married to one woman while taking irresponsible pleasure in countless others before or after her. This is the Islamic perspective.

Many Middle Eastern women see Western practices as abusive to the psyches of Western women. For example, the growing use of plastic surgery in Western countries is disturbing to them. Middle Eastern women are covered in public, so their physical appearance and beauty do not come into question in their self-image or self-esteem. A Muslim woman's beauty is something to be revealed only to those who are in her innermost circle; not just anyone can partake in that event. Thus, a Muslim woman's sexuality and physical appearance is not at all the basis for how she is seen in the society. Our self-esteem comprises all the factors that we are praised, admired, and despised for.

In Western societies, women are scrutinized and critically looked upon for their physical beauty and appearance. Our television media, the film industry, and magazines all demand it from us. We must have the right rear, legs, chest, and waistline. This is not a simple matter of a natural desire to look good; women are expected to attend to every aspect of their physical appearance with great fervor and zeal. According to Eastern women who are driven by the principles of their value system, which place emphasis and value on the nobility of their character, the fact that women feel the need to surgically enlarge their bosoms or undergo other painful and invasive procedures to enhance their physical appearance is evidence of the oppression of Western women.

The Western community has many stereotypes about Eastern women, and vice versa. Middle Eastern women do not enjoy exactly the same freedoms that Westerners do, just as Middle Eastern men do not enjoy exactly the same freedoms that Western men do. The East and the West are two different societies with different principles and value systems. Neither is necessarily better than the other; they are just different. Comparing the two systems quickly brings out the realization that good analogies can't be made between disparate value systems. We are comparing apples and oranges.

Of course, Eastern women have a long way to go in many areas, but while it is easy for Westerners to pick out various examples of oppression in the East, it is similarly easy for Easterners to find examples of oppression of women in the West. Because East and West come from two totally different cultural contexts, such judgments can obscure more important problems. A Western woman might find it oppressive that an Eastern woman is pressured to dress conservatively, and conclude that it is because her sexuality is being unnaturally constrained and preserved only for the use of men. The Eastern woman might find it similarly oppressive that the Western woman feels compelled to spend a lot of time and money on makeup and stylish clothes. She might conclude that the Western woman's self-esteem depends unnaturally on an appearance of wealth and sexual attractiveness rather than on the quality of her moral character, and that she will have a hard time being taken seriously as a result. Either of these judgments seem perfectly reasonable depending on your cultural context.

Unfortunately, these kinds of issues also distract us from much more serious matters, such as equal access to education, health care, and basic human rights. In the case of Afghanistan, we must first make sure that women are safe, fed, and healthy and that they have the right to earn a livelihood. Their appearance should not skirt this inherent and basic human right. They are people with real feelings, intuitions, and needs that are too easily clouded by their dress and appearance.

❦

The nature of marriage in Eastern societies is one that is easily misunderstood by Westerners. In Afghan culture, marriage is very much structured by tradition. Even for Afghans who live in the U.S., it continues to be highly regarded institution. It is based on values that Afghans hold dear. It is not treated as a casual commitment by those who enter it. In addition to being the system by which families are joined together and built upon, it is the process by which a girl ascends to womanhood, garnering all the respect and accepting all the responsibilities that rightfully belong to an Afghan woman.

In the Western system, the standard idea of a marriage proposal involves a man bending down on one knee with an engagement ring before his girlfriend, who decides whether or not she wants to accept. Of course, American couples' engagement rituals vary widely; however, it is usually a private, personal event between the future bride and groom. In the Afghan system, the proposal revolves heavily around the couple's families. Even in cases when two people have bonded in a personal relationship and have decided to make a marriage commitment, they are not able to do so until the man's family formally asks the woman's family for her hand in marriage.

Traditional Afghan men and women usually meet at school or at community functions, but more modern Afghans meet where anyone else would, including such places as nightclubs. If a man and woman become interested in each other, they keep their attraction secret. They usually spark some sort of relationship on the telephone or now on the Internet, where they spend endless amounts of time getting to know each other. Eventually they will see each other in a public place. In Afghanistan, that public place would be an occasion for the two to exchange glances only; after the event, they could then talk on the phone all night. In the West, Afghan couples take a much more open approach: They go out to public places to talk and get to know each other, but always secretively, and always at places where they pray that nobody from the community will see them!

The courtship process usually begins with a suitor's family coming to the young woman's home, without the suitor himself, for afternoon tea with her family. The hosting woman's family normally does not serve any sweet items that might indicate agreement with the proposal, even if they are prepared to agree to it. The man's family generally starts by making small talk to try to get to know the other family a little better.

At this time, the woman being courted makes a quick appearance by coming out of her room to greet the guests. Under normal circumstances this should be the first time that the suitor's family formally meets her, although the proposing suitor obviously has seen her and likes her well enough to make a formal proposal to her family. In some families, the courted woman will also serve tea and then move swiftly to another room, usually her bedroom. She stays in the room for the rest of the visit, as the rest of the conversation will pertain to her and her marriage, which is considered an inappropriate topic to be brought up in front of her. Naturally, her family will fill her in when the guests leave, unless she is listening from behind the door.

The process normally includes tracing family heritage lines so that both families can pinpoint the exact regions of Afghanistan they are from. They also discuss other specifics about education level, financial security, and so forth. After having done so, the man's family will officially proclaim their intention of coming to the woman's house for the purpose of marriage, and will begin to paint a heavenly picture of their prized son in order to gain the favor of the woman's parents.

Even if the woman's family and the woman herself agree to this, it is considered unseemly to accept or show any signs of interest on the first visit. The man's family must show great effort and make the attempt a few more times. The idea is to make the man's family work hard for her hand in marriage, as her parents are not willing to give up their esteemed daughter easily.

After the man's family leaves, the woman and her mother alone usually discuss the gentleman caller and his family, as it is not considered appropriate for a young woman to talk about such things with her father. The mother will relay the daughter's opinions to the father afterward.

If the daughter's feelings are favorable, her father and mother begin an investigation. They contact various members of the Afghan community who are familiar with the suitor and his family and who can provide significant, detailed facts on their history, background, and all other information pertinent to the decision. Even if the woman has already decided that she wants to marry her suitor, her family will still conduct a background check to ensure his suitability. If all goes well, her family will announce a date when the suitor and his family can pick up the *shirni*, or candy, which is symbolic of their decision to say yes.

On the day of the giving of the shirni, the woman's family prepares a meal for the suitor, who shows up with a whole entourage of close family members—mother, father, sisters and brothers, uncles and aunts. The suitor's family is then presented with a beautiful gold or silver tray that carries a matching wrapped box of chocolate, decorated beautifully with flowers, colorful and shiny candies, or the Afghan sugar-coated almond candy called *nuqul*, all wrapped up in sheer fabric of various designs. Some will also include in the tray some fabric intricately embroidered with gold or silver thread, or sometimes even real gemstones such as rubies and emeralds.

The woman is brought into the room where the event is taking place only after the shirni is given. Upon entering the room, she is officially engaged. She is presented with a promise token, usually an emerald or ruby ring. She then sits with her new fiancé and together they watch his family pick up the tray of candy and dance with it to show their excitement and joy at the momentous occasion and honor that has been bestowed on them.

The event is usually fairly short, only a few hours long, and includes only close family members who participate in the formal function. At the end, the man's family takes the tray of shirni with them. Later they return just the tray with cash that is intended to help the woman's family pay for the subsequent engagement party, which will include all family, relatives, friends, and so forth. It is not expected that the woman's parents will both marry their daughter away and incur the entire expense of the engagement party.

At the engagement party, which is hosted by the woman's family, the bride-to-be traditionally wears the color pink. Most women end up having dresses custom made. The hosts have to do a great deal of footwork to gather all of the necessary ingredients for the party, such as long sugar cones (*Qand*) and fancy *Banarasi* fabric from India that covers the couch on which the engaged couple will be seated. Most Afghans throw large engagement parties with elaborate Afghan cuisine, live Afghan singers, flowers galore, and all of the factors that usually go into an American wedding reception. It is at this party that the diamond engagement ring is placed on the bride's finger. The bride is also given a set of precious jewelry that includes a necklace, earrings, ring, and bracelet, as well as several outfits with matching shoes and purses to wear during her engagement period.

Following this party, plans for the wedding commence. The groom's family pays for the wedding. Afghan weddings involve a great deal of detail and work, particularly in the United States, as it is difficult to find hotels that allow outside caterers who can provide authentic Afghan cuisine and which can accommodate a party that runs to after one or two o'clock in the morning. In addition, a royal green dress must be purchased for the bride to wear at her wedding ceremony. It is only following the ceremony, at the reception, that she will wear the typical white wedding dress of her choice.

The wedding ceremony is usually attended by close family members. It is a serious event where the marriage contract is agreed upon. In this ceremony, the bride can either speak on her own behalf or appoint a spokesperson to represent her interests, as if she were royalty. The religious leader who performs the ceremony will ask some questions to ensure the identity and lawfulness of the marriage. Even more important, the dowry must be agreed upon. Sometimes this issue becomes quite controversial when families have not previously discussed and agreed upon it. Conflicts can arise when the bride's family wants to raise the amount of the dowry and the groom can't afford it. In any event, this process takes place in order to officiate the marriage between the bride and groom according to Islamic laws.

Following the ceremony, at the reception, a stage is set up where the bride and groom sit. Their area includes a variety of elements that often prove difficult to find. The couch that the bride and groom sit on must be draped with an expensive silk fabric adorned with silver or gold threadwork. A low table will be set before them on which to place candelabras, a basket full of henna, a punch bowl or beautiful pitcher to hold the *sharbat* or juice for the newlyweds to drink (not alcohol, which is forbidden in Islam), and flute glasses. These are the essential components, although some people add more detail to their tables.

In a ceremony during the reception, a decorative shawl is placed above the bride and groom, and a mirror in which no one has ever looked is slipped under the shawl for the bride and groom to see each other in. This tradition dates back to the time of arranged marriages, when the bride and groom actually saw each other for the first time in that mirror. Following this, an appointed member of the family places henna on the palms of the bride and groom and then covers their palms with designed fabrics made exclusively for them to use. The fabric keeps the henna from getting messy. It takes about an hour to stain the hands of the newlyweds bright orange.

Sitting on a riser above the crowd places the bride and groom in the spotlight; they are king and queen for the evening. The guests dance before them and entertain them as best they can. It makes the bride and groom feel that this is the biggest night of their lives, where they are deserving of honor and privilege.

The morning after the wedding, the newlyweds attend a brunch traditionally held by the groom's family. The bride's family sends either catered or home-cooked Afghan specialty foods to the brunch, although they do not actually attend. The purpose of the event is to acquaint the new bride with her husband's family and to allow them to welcome her. The bride wears a white dress that is suitable for a daytime brunch event.

Following the wedding, a series of parties that includes the extended family takes place in honor of the newly married couple, and the host gives the bride a piece of jewelry at each of those parties. At the first party given by the groom's family, the new bride customarily wears a red dress. Depending on the size of the families, these parties can last for an entire year's worth of weekends, and they usually cost the bride many pounds gained from delicious late-night Afghan dinners.

≈ ≈

My dad used to explain to me that there was a natural connection between two people who shared the same cultural background that simply couldn't occur with outsiders. He told me that marriage was hard enough without the problems inherent in merging disparate cultures. He would repeat an old Afghan adage: "Pigeons fly with pigeons as crows fly with crows; the same breed flies with the same breed." He felt that the commingling of different "breeds" was simply unnatural, and people who did so defied the laws of nature.

I tried to convince him that by differentiating among "breeds," he was equating human beings with animals, as if we were dogs to be matched up by pedigree. It seemed quite clear to me that humans are humans, and individuals can only be thought of as better or worse based on their moral standing and the substance of their character, not on how pure their bloodlines are. The usual reply was that I was wrong and he was right, and that I would be disowned by my family if I were to ever marry anyone who was not Afghan.

I now realize that his insistence on marrying Afghans was not based on a simple preference for "purity" but on a survival mechanism. My father is very conscious of the fact that Afghans are the largest refugee group in the world and that to preserve our heritage, language, and so forth, we do not have the luxury of marrying whomever we please based on normal circumstances. Our circumstances are far from normal. His nationalism stems from a desire to ensure our Afghan legacy.

But at the time this seemed harsh, especially since I thought there were no Afghans in my league. I was one of the oldest first-generation Afghan-Americans in my community, as my parents were among the first to leave Afghanistan, prior to the Soviet war. The Afghan boys in my age group were fairly new immigrants who either had old-fashioned ways or were trying quite transparently to play the American role, with mannerisms that seemed foreign to me. They generally fell into two extremes: either too rough and ungentlemanly, expecting their wives to tap-dance around their tempers, wants, and needs, or overly romantic pushovers who would surely take anything I threw at them. None was a challenge worth pursuing.

Some suitors were under the impression that an A-list education was all it took to gain the hand of the bride of their choice. But I knew that no matter how many academic degrees a man might have framed on his wall, if I could not see eye to eye with him, the relationship would fall apart. There were plenty of Afghans in our community who had gained the documentation that proved they were educated, yet who did not have the character traits, class, or demeanor that one would expect from an educated person. The man I eventually chose to marry did not have his bachelor's degree, and many of my former suitors' parents were aghast that I had rejected their sons with master's and doctoral degrees for such a person. Once such woman approached me at a social event. I thought she was going to congratulate me on my engagement, but instead she told me that I was a fool for choosing Samir over her own son, who had a doctorate: "Everybody thought that with all of your rejections, you would surely end up with at least a doctor or a lawyer!"

For that move I became the talk of the town for a while, but it actually ended up defusing a lot of the tension and hostility that these parents harbored toward me—it made them feel better about themselves that I had not refused their sons based on their level of educational achievement. I believed that if I wanted a doctorate then I should earn one myself, rather than trying to take credit for one through my husband.

What everyone didn't seem to understand was that my intention was to marry someone who was principle-based, honest, soft, sincere, simple, genuine, uncomplicated (since I was complicated enough for both of us), kind, and dignified. I was searching for one of those "ideal Afghans" that I had learned about to become part of my life and to complete my identity—someone who was *aseel*, genuine and authentic. His degree, job title, and car were not on my list of priorities, since I was capable of acquiring these on my own. In sum, I was looking for a rare commodity. Even if some Afghan men had some of these qualities, they would lack others.

It seemed like an impossible feat to find such a man within the small, close-knit local Afghan community.

Mothers in the community who wanted to find a wife for their sons would scope out Afghan girls, shamelessly obvious about getting a good look at our figures and faces. If they liked what they saw, they would sit next to us or ask us to come and sit next to them, asking us our names and what families we were from. The first time this happened to me was at a dinner party I attended with my parents when I was still in junior high school! Perhaps I looked older than my age. But many older Afghan women who are worried about the openness of American society prefer younger girls, whom they believe are more likely to be virgins; the status of the older ones starts to get iffy.

This particular woman who approached me was scouting out girls for her prized son, and began to ask me a series of questions that became progressively more personal. She actually asked me what my father did for a living, and if we owned our home or were renting. I thought the conversation was getting awfully personal for someone I didn't even know. I couldn't believe my ears when she asked me what my father's salary was! At this point I was getting a kick out of her audacity. I told her that I didn't know — which was the truth, as my parents never discussed finances around their children. She then asked for my address. I just told her the city I lived in, hoping that would be enough. But she got our address and telephone number from a friend of my parents. Then the drama began.

This woman began to call my mom, hounding her to come over for tea. My mother politely dismissed her. She told her, "My daughter intends to study now and isn't interested in marrying anyone. It's really nothing personal." Then, one day as I walked home from the school bus stop, I noticed a pair of strange women leaving my house. My mother was at work at this time of day, so who could they be? One looked familiar, and I realized that it was the nosy woman from the dinner party.

I jumped behind a tree to hide from them, but they spotted me. My heart dropped. I was all alone and didn't know how to handle these much older people. After we said hello, I told them that my parents weren't at home and tried to excuse myself. But the sister of the "gentleman caller" was quite persistent. She began to tell me some pretty creative stories about her brother being a regular Rico Suave.

Luckily, my mom happened to call home in the middle of this. My little sister came out of the house and told me that she wanted to speak to me. I went inside and told my mom that these women were here and that they were being very pushy. My mother lost her cool. She told me to put them on the phone. I listened as they tried to bargain with my mom for another chance. They must have assumed that we were playing hard to get. But then my mother made some kind of remark to them that silenced them. I'm not sure what it was, but that was the last I ever saw of those two women.

Many years later, when I was twenty-one years old, living at home and going to college, a young man's aunt spotted me at my cousin's engagement party. The man's family contacted my mother and proceeded to visit our house to formally propose as suitors at an afternoon tea. Traditionally, on the first visit, only the suitor's family comes to tea. However, in this case, the candidate himself accompanied his family, with my mother's approval.

I had not yet seen or met the suitor, so I really had no interest in the whole ordeal. My dad was angry that my mom had agreed to this arrangement, as it was assumed that they would be rejected anyway. Oddly enough, the suitor, Samir, had no interest in the ordeal either, as he didn't have much confidence in his aunt's taste. But it turned out that Samir's father had been a neighbor of my mother's family; they had grown up on the same block in Kabul. Because of my mom's affinity towards his father's family, she allowed the tea to take place in Samir's presence. She was just curious to see what had become of the son of the boy next door after all these years.

I was annoyed at the whole situation. It took place during the month of fasting, Ramadan, and I wanted to focus on my spirituality, not scope out a guy. In any event, I did not take the visit seriously and brushed it off even while they were at the house. When the family called after their visit, I told my mom to flatly reject them.

Fate has a strange way of unfolding. The family continued to court. Samir's sister persisted in gaining permission for him to call and in trying to get me to at least give him a fair shot before rejecting him out of hand. I was determined to bring things to a close right then and there, but after he called I found myself unable to reject him and was in fact intrigued by his conversation, his genuine attitude, and his demeanor.

Samir and I gradually got to know each other better over the telephone. Eventually he asked that we see each other in person, though I still felt that there was no point since this would not end up in marriage. But when finally we met for dinner, it seemed that the person I saw was someone other than the one I had met that afternoon in Ramadan.

Since he had invited me out, we agreed to meet at an Italian restaurant of his choice. The drive felt like an eternity. I was incredibly nervous and wondered why I had agreed to this. Each of the many times that I checked my appearance in the rearview mirror, I asked my reflection, "What are you doing?"

I arrived at the restaurant at the same time as he did, and we walked in together. It struck me: How could I possibly eat in front of him? When we sat down, Samir seemed very comfortable. He was confident and bold, not shy and awkward as I had thought — and he was quite handsome, I might add. My original notion that this would not work soon faded. Several months later, we were engaged.

Miraculously, Samir fit the mold of a husband that I had constructed in my mind. Before meeting him, I was caught between my own conflicting desires: those of being Islamically conscious and adhering to parental and cultural expectations, and those of Southern Californian society at large. Samir managed to make me feel so normal, rather than out of place as either too Americanized, too traditional, too Islamically inclined, too hot, too cold, too whatever. Further, he was Afghan. Though he has a fair complexion and looks European or American, he is from the southern part of Afghanistan and speaks the native language of Pashto as well as Dari. His Pashtun cultural background automatically helped qualify him in many of the areas I had set out in my mind as desirable in a husband. This is not to say that these characteristics are found exclusively in Pashtun Afghans, but it certainly was the case with Samir. The tendencies toward honor, principle, dignity, and no-nonsense straightforwardness were all in place. The right combination of being soft and reasonably even-tempered while not being a pushover, the kindheartedness, and all the rest were evident and encapsulated in one person.

After we became engaged, the wedding plans began. It was strenuous to work so closely on a task so arduous with a group of people that I hardly knew. It was made more difficult because I — like most brides — was the one who was most particular about how things would take shape, but I wasn't in control of the wedding finances, since the groom's family traditionally pays. Since they were to incur all the costs, all of my decisions would first have to go through them. I quickly learned that my tastes would require a substantial amount of money, but as a wedding comes only once, I felt it was important to do everything right. The traditional Afghan bride usually allows the groom's family to simply present her with the ring and take care of all parts of the wedding, but I had not been raised to accept such a gesture on perhaps one of the most important occasions of life. I was an Afghan-American, and I wanted to create a synthesis between the Afghan code and what I have come to know as true in America. It was a tremendous challenge dealing with near strangers on the intimate details of my wedding.

When an Afghan bride has acquainted herself with her fiancé on her own, she usually does not have much leverage in gaining additional support from the groom's family in certain areas, including their expected wedding expenditures. This is because the family of the groom feels that a girl who has agreed to marriage herself—for example, if she meets the groom independently and pursues a relationship that later leads to a marriage commitment—is already "guaranteed" and not subject to the risk of being "lost." She is not as highly esteemed, due to the lack of pursuit on the part of the family. But because I was sought by the suitor and his family in the most traditional sense, I had more leverage. There was no strong guarantee that I would commit to the marriage. Even after the engagement there was a sense that it was still a time of getting to know one another, and circumstances might yet lead in the opposite direction. In this situation, the groom's family generally avoids rocking the boat, at least until they are sure that there is no chance of losing the girl of their choice—sometimes not a sure thing until after the birth of the first child.

This concept of pursuit is key to the treatment of women in Afghan relationships. Even when the family of the groom comes to the home of the bride to propose marriage, the suitors are not treated or spoken to in an open and comfortable manner. They are kept in suspense as to the decision of the woman's family, even if they are certain that the woman wishes to accept the proposal. It is expected that the bride's family will play hard-to-get with the groom's family. When a suitor's family goes to the woman's home to make the marriage proposal, if they are not turned down on the first try, then her family will seem desperate for a marriage. Often, suitors are either not given concrete answers or even rejected at first. They are expected to play the part of insisting and persisting on several trips to the bride-to-be's home until they have exhausted the family into saying yes, reluctantly.

There is no purchase of a ring or any other formal commitment until it is officially approved by both families. It is only after this approval that the woman will be engaged or married. In the event that her family does not approve of the suitor, she must either concede to them or reject her family's wishes and proceed regardless of their decision. However, once again, such a woman would not be held in the highest of esteem, since the concept of pursuit has been lost. She will be seen in a lower light than women who participate in the process in a more traditional fashion.

Once the family of the groom has worked hard to attain their new bride, or *arous*, she is expected to take on important responsibilities, just as a daughter would do for her own parents—and always with a smile. This would be the case even if the groom's family didn't spend a fortune on her with jewelry, clothes, and parties. The duties she is expected to perform might include taking her husband's mother and father to their doctors' appointments or welcoming them with wonderful home-cooked meals any time they decide to pop over for a visit (assuming she is not actually living with her in-laws). Sleepovers are a favorite custom of in-laws, so she should be prepared to set aside her weekend or whatever days they decide to visit, as they expect her full attention. Such visits are not usually planned in advance or arranged with the daughter-in-law. Since the couple's home is seen as their son's home, permission or formal notification is not required. There are many other subtle expectations of respect and hospitality (*Ehteram wa Ezzat*) that sometimes prove to be cumbersome, especially for someone who is not brought up in that culture and wants to think she married just her husband, not his whole family.

Shortly after the wedding, the groom's family usually expects to see a grandchild. Daughters-in-law are generally urged to have one child soon after the wedding while they are young, partly to prove that they are capable of bearing children and partly to solidify the marriage. After the first child, they are usually free to have the rest of their children later if they desire, according to their own plans. From my personal observations, I have found that the strong desire among Afghan in-laws for the couple to have children has a lot to do with sealing the commitment of marriage between the marriage partners. I sense that as a woman grows more educated and financially independent, her in-laws feel insecure if there are no children to ground her in the marriage. She could simply pick up and leave without losing anything significant.

Although I was born and raised in the United States, it turned out that every aspect of my courtship, engagement, and wedding adhered to the traditional customs of Afghanistan. It was certainly more traditional than my own parents' marriage. The fact that I was able to find a compatible husband by following the traditional route all the way through, and therefore to be held in the high esteem that is essential to the success of Afghan marriages, makes me reconsider the wisdom of such arrangements that I used to mock so profusely.

I think the reason I mocked them was because I bought into the stereotype that tradition is automatically the same thing as being backward. But the point of tradition is to enrich life. If used properly, it is enriching; if used improperly, it can strip people of their individuality. Understanding is key. The essence of growing up is to see through appearances and discover the true purpose behind the systems that guide our lives. I realized that maturation is the process of seeking genuine understanding rather than accepting out of hand what we think we already know. As a woman, it meant taking a fresh look at the role that cultural traditions played in my journey to adulthood. As a Muslim, it meant growing from a nominal belief in Islam into real faith.

⚜ Seven ⚜

The Real Islam

I took my first trip to the mosque when I was ten years old. My father wanted me to take classes there on reading the Quran. It was the first time my dad ever told me to cover my hair, and my mom gave me one of her scarves. They told me not to wear my shorts but to dress in pants or a skirt.

I was nervous about the whole ordeal, and when I went into the mosque that nervousness grew exponentially. Children were busily practicing reading the Quran for when it would be their turn to read in front of the teacher. The teacher was Ezzatullah Mujadidi, who turned out to be the brother of a former president of Afghanistan, Subghatullah Mujadidi. He seemed very large to me. In his hand he held a long, beautiful silver pen, which he repeatedly tapped on the book when a student paused to sound out the syllables of the Arabic words in the Quran.

One boy in the group who was a lot older than everyone else just couldn't seem to pronounce or read properly. At one particular show of bad performance, Mujadidi struck him. The boy's mother, who was there to help out with the class, was strongly offended and burst into tears. I was absolutely fear-stricken, and I thanked God a million times that my grandmother had made me practice all of those miserable days at home learning the alphabet and sounding out words to read. Mujadidi was insulted at the mother's lack of appreciation of his services, put his things in his sleek black briefcase, and took off for the parking lot. The boy's father ran after him and pleaded for him to come back.

Mr. Mujadidi did return, and then it was my turn to read. I smiled at him to gain his acceptance, and he asked me my name. I said "Maryam." He asked what my father's name was. I said "Qadeer." He quickly said, "Abdul Qadeer jaan," correcting the informal manner in which I had referred to my father.

He placed a book in front of me that I was very familiar with from my grandmother's forced lessons. He asked me to begin, so I read the very best I could. I saw that speed was important to him, because I had to keep up with the swift strokes of his pen as it moved from the right to the left side of the page. Luckily, I made no mistakes and didn't pause even once. He was very pleased with me. He loudly said, "You see, this is the kind of student I like — one who has done her homework!" I was so relieved to have won his approval. A surge of energy swept through me. Then I brattily gave the teenage boy an arrogant look for his incompetence, and sat down to learn something else that I could impress my new teacher with.

I noticed that the mosque was filled with people of all sorts of nationalities. It was the first time I realized that Afghans were not the only Muslims. Women of other cultures adopted the modest dress in different ways: some in chic suits, others in long coats, yet others in black burqa-type dresses. Some of them wore colorful Indian saris with matching scarves. I noticed that these Indo-Pakistani women had a specific fondness for gold jewelry, as they were adorned in it from head to toe.

I felt a sense of peace and comfort in the mosque despite the high expectations of my teacher, and I grew quite attached to it. However, eventually my teacher moved to another state, and my interest in the classes fizzled out. I didn't go back to the mosque after that until I was in high school. Yet I still see my first teacher, Mr. Mujadidi, at Afghan community functions on occasion, and when I do I always pay my respects to him. He has earned my respect because he has given me knowledge. I am indebted to him for what he taught me—not only letters and words, but the whole learning experience.

In Islamic tradition, teachers are of high caliber and enjoy the loyalty and respect of all their students as well as of the society at large. When Muslims pray, they pray for their teachers after praying for their parents. In Afghanistan, when governments changed hands and various people were executed, many teachers were spared because their loyal students were in the army or occupied other key positions and refused to bite the hand that had fed them. Normally teachers are paid very little or not at all, but they are surrounded by disciples for life. Over the course of several years of teaching, these respectful former students grow into quite a large number, which accords the teacher a great deal of prestige. As one person put it to me, "Your student might go on to become the president of the United States—but when he gets a call from his teacher, that's one call he takes!"

During my teenage spiritual resurgence, I returned to the mosque to attend a women's group that conducted study sessions on the Quran. We spent evenings picking apart sections of the Quran to probe its meaning. A teacher was always present to give us substantive direction, without which we would have been simply hypothesizing in the dark. It was a wonderful way to bond with the other women as well as with the community at large. Adults came together at the mosque to steer its course and organize its growth. Older boys and girls in the youth group planned spiritual retreats. Younger children aspired to be members of that illustrious youth group one day.

Eventually I was recommended to teach children's classes. During these classes, I tried to instill in the children the difference between Muslim people, their cultures and politics, and the religion of Islam. One little girl had lost her watch in the mosque, and was so distraught that it hadn't been turned in that she stopped coming to the mosque altogether. I found it so ridiculous—why would she want to disassociate from an entire religion because of one person's individual actions?

After that, whenever I taught a lesson from the textbook such as the pilgrimage to the Ka'aba in Mecca, I closed with some of the "real" things that happen there. For instance, I told them that despite it being a sacred place and people claiming to sincerely observe the rituals, many people are robbed or mugged there. Others are pushed and shoved as people try to get closer to the Ka'aba to touch it. Then I asked them, "Will this make you blame Islam, or just the shady people who do these things?" The kids said, "Those people, of course." Then they told me about their innovative schemes to place mousetraps around their waists where they kept their money belts so that if someone were to grab them, they would get their fingers caught. My sister would tell me I was going overboard by saying things like that, but I didn't care, because I wanted to be sure that none of my students would ever succumb to such a shallow outlook.

After class, the children lined up in the prayer hall to join the congregation for the group evening prayer. Beautifully colored, ornate prayer rugs were placed on the floor for the Muslims to prostrate themselves on as they literally bowed to Almighty God. Then the muezzin said the call to prayer, in a heavenly voice that sounded so serene and pleasant to my ears.

At the mosque I noticed an awkward man who sat in an office counting stacks of money—that is all I ever saw him do. One day, I decided that I wanted to purchase a copy of the Quran with an English translation, and I was told to go and see him. When I asked him how much it cost for the book, he said that the Quran had no price tag and was invaluable. He said that the mosque simply took whatever a person could afford to pay, and took nothing at all if a person could not.

I said, "Is twenty dollars all right?"

"Whatever you can afford," he replied.

"Forty?"

"Whatever you can afford," he repeated.

I quickly gave him the forty dollars for fear that if I continued, he would drain my entire allowance.

There is no defined "membership" to mosques; you can go to whichever one you choose. Despite the Sunni and Shiite sects, there are no formal distinctions among interpretations or levels of orthodoxy such as those that exist in Christianity or Judaism. However, different mosques do attract different kinds of people. Some mosques are dominated by a single ethnic group, while others are characterized as liberal or conservative.

I have now found a mosque that I am very comfortable with, but at first I tried going to different mosques because I didn't want to be closed off from any particular one. I listened to and spoke with different groups of Muslims who felt differently, sometimes quite strongly, about various issues. I tried to stay out of the politics of the community. I learned what I could from the knowledge that people had to offer, and left how they conducted their personal lives or views to themselves. I was certainly not in a position to judge, nor did I want to be judged. By being open to different ideas, I was able to sample the rich flavor of the Muslim community in California.

Some months prior to the September 11 attacks, a roving Taliban ambassador by the name of Rahmatullah Hashimi came to the U.S. and made many appearances at universities and on radio and television programs. He was a well-spoken, well-mannered gentleman who tried to explain and justify the practices of his government to Western audiences. It was from him that I realized how black-and-white the world was to the Taliban. They did not allow themselves to complicate their outlook in ways that might compromise the success of their goals, which were to gain full authority over the people who needed to be subdued into safety and security. They plainly believed that they were the only group able to pacify the country, and the fact that they did so was a testament to the soundness of their methods. They believed that they were working in the interest of the people, as evidenced by the progress they had made in safeguarding the country from its prior turmoil.

I attended a talk that Hashimi gave at my university, where he addressed a mostly American audience. He was a short, serious man in his early twenties, already married with children, and quite self-confident. He had deep green eyes and wore a turban with the traditional Afghani dress.

Hashimi began his discussion by clarifying that Afghanistan is not a Western society, and that its practices cannot be assessed in relation to the practices of the West. They could not reasonably be compared. So far, so good, I thought. He moved on to explain some of the mannerisms of the East, which do not promote boasting or "public-relations measures," as he put it. Hashimi was trying to show that the Taliban was not accustomed to drawing attention to their strengths nor engaging in superficial diplomatic relations in order to justify themselves. They felt no need to justify their ways to the West or any others, as they controlled a sovereign state that prided itself on having a civilization that had existed since ancient times.

When asked, Hashimi did explain many of the accomplishments of the Taliban, such as the safety and security they managed to bring to a country that had otherwise been in total chaos. He appealed to the Westerners to tolerate their practices relative not to the Western context, but to the Eastern, Afghan context. For instance, he cited the burqa as an old Afghan practice that the Taliban did not create but simply reinstituted. Many women of Afghanistan wore burqas even during the country's most liberal era. When challenged about the Taliban's practices, he stated that either his word could be accepted at face value or he would extend an invitation to Afghanistan so people could see for themselves that what they were hearing here was mere propaganda.

The session with Hashimi was short, and I had many questions for him, so I approached him afterward. I asked him about Osama bin Laden's threat to the security of Afghanistan. At this point, the U.S. and United Nations were calling on Afghanistan to give up bin Laden for his role in previous terrorist attacks. Bin Laden was not an Afghan and had plenty of money to live anywhere he pleased. Why was he allowed to remain in the country when it jeopardized the safety and welfare of the already impoverished Afghan population?

Hashimi simply replied that because I was born in the United States, I did not understand. He said that bin Laden had taken shelter with the Afghans, fought with them side by side in the war with the Soviets, and was a guest of the Afghans. Therefore, they could not morally turn him away. When I replied that he was endangering the lives of millions of Afghans, he responded that bin Laden was not guilty of anything and was being used as a scapegoat. The Taliban had repeatedly requested that the U.S. supply them with proof of his guilt—a request that the U.S. flatly refused, according to Hashimi. He further noted that Afghanistan was an Islamic nation with its own set of guidelines and judicial proceedings. He said that the Taliban had tried to cooperate with America's requests and that if they were supplied with proof of bin Laden's guilt, they would turn him over to a third-party, neutral, Islamic country, to be tried in an Islamic court. However, it would be impossible for the Taliban to turn over a Muslim guest who was thought to be innocent to a non-Muslim nation for prosecution when there was no evidence of his guilt.

Hashimi's words about bin Laden's status as a "guest" of Afghanistan have particular importance in Afghan culture. The Afghan codes of pride (*ghaiyrat*) and hospitality (*ezzat*) are key to Afghan identity. Ghaiyrat compels Afghans to behave in accordance with a strict code of honor. They will often sacrifice their own self-interest to uphold the principles of that code.

Afghans are renowned for their hospitality. Even a total stranger who shows up at the door of an Afghan will be met with a warm greeting and endless care and generosity, especially if he or she is an outsider. In fact, Afghans are taught that even if your enemy comes to your home, you must receive him or her with hospitality. It is highly dishonorable to turn someone away from your home, regardless of the circumstances. After someone has left your home, then you can pick any bones of contention, but not while the person is under your roof—not if you are a true Afghan.

Afghans are bound to this code of honor and are willing to die to uphold it. To a true Afghan, you might as well be dead if you live a life without honor, pride, and dignity. Someone who takes refuge with an Afghan can actually stake a claim to protection, loyalty, and hospitality without conditions or expectations for reciprocity. So if you're on the run, an Afghan is your best ticket to unquestioned protection and loyalty. Naturally, this can easily be taken advantage of by less scrupulous guests. It puts Afghans in a precarious position to hold honor above self-preservation.

However, this does not mean that any guilty criminal or fugitive can take shelter in an Afghan's home. But a person will always be presumed innocent until proven guilty. Naturally, a sheltered guest's enemies could come to proffer stories of guilt. If it is in fact shown that the person is guilty of the accused crimes, then only upon assurance of his guilt will he be released. Even then, he will be released to protect himself on his own, not necessarily to his captors. When the Taliban refused to hand over Osama bin Laden to Western authorities after September 11, they claim that they were basing their actions at least partly on this principle of ghaiyrat.

Afghans feel that the moral awareness that arises from ghaiyrat separates them from the rest of human civilization. While others sell each other out, true Afghans who practice this honor code feel a great sense of dignity and spiritual richness. It gives them their air of confidence and depth and their pure, no-nonsense attitude. It enables them to project a healthy pride despite the political failures and socioeconomic downfalls that they have endured.

Against this background of the principles that Afghans hold

dear to their hearts, Ambassador Hashimi's explanations about why the Taliban allowed bin Laden to remain in Afghanistan as their guest seemed somewhat reasonable, though illogical. Certainly, it seemed reasonable that they should exercise their principles and ghaiyrat. But it was illogical when it would cost them their government and the lives of so many innocent civilian Afghans. Hashimi did say that bin Laden should realize that he was jeopardizing our nation and ought to do the right thing by leaving so that his host would not be in harm's way. But bin Laden was unreasonable, according to Hashimi, and would not offer to leave on his own. Hashimi said, "We certainly can't kick him out. Where will he go?"

Nonetheless, I implored him to exercise his diplomatic expertise to strike a deal that would end the bin Laden conflict. I suggested that he should try to achieve some sort of diplomatic resolution in Washington, where he was going to visit in a few days, for the sake of the people. A government must uphold the greatest good for the greatest number — and protecting one man when it places a whole country in jeopardy is not morally justifiable. But Hashimi simply replied that the West needed to mind its own affairs and let the East mind its own. He closed by saying that the United States was based on an entirely different value system that could not be imposed upon the East, which has minded its own affairs for thousands of years. He believed that there would be no real dialogue or open exchange between countries that had little in common ideologically.

Some weeks later, while Hashimi was still in town, the Taliban scheduled the demolition of the Bamiyan Buddhist statues. Hashimi's explanation for this was that UN-backed agencies were spending a great deal of money on the preservation of the ancient Buddha statues. The Taliban approached these agencies and asked them to allocate some of the funds being spent on the stone statues to the living Afghan children who were dying of starvation. Scores of beautiful Afghan kids were literally dying by the hour, so why not spend some money to save life rather than stone? Their request was flatly denied. The angered Taliban then decided to destroy the statues and thereby cut off aid for their preservation, since they deemed them no more valuable than the poor children of the country who were orphaned, cold, homeless, hungry, and dying. There were real-life human beings whose deaths could be spared by the aid that was being poured into the stone statues; this is what angered the Taliban, according to Hashimi. The Taliban did not use common diplomatic measures in any of their conflicts or disagreements, but instead took drastic measures to show how they resented the West's treatment of their country as well as their expectation that the world should not interfere in their ways.

❦ ❦

The Taliban captured the world's attention with their atrocities and oppressive practices. They have since been accused of placing women in a subservient position to men. They are hated for executing, in the infamous soccer stadium, people who were suspected of a crime. The Taliban have been accused of harboring terrorists, and they are reviled for their retrogressive doctrine.

But we must look at the source of this state of Afghan affairs and should not forget the real monster, which crumbled a perfectly functional country and turned it into a Pandora's box from which all forms of evil flow. The Taliban would never have had a place in Afghanistan had it not been for the Soviet war. The Soviets set into motion the domino effect of widespread destruction that has reached as far as the twin towers in New York.

It cannot be emphasized enough that the Taliban is not representative of Afghans or Muslims. The Taliban was a regime primarily led by poorly educated zealots who were not qualified to lead a nation. The doctrine that they followed has its roots not in authentic Islam nor even in traditional interpretations of Islam but in the Deobandi school founded in 1867 in India.[1] The Taliban's actions painted Afghans and Muslims alike as terrorist barbarians; the Pashtun Afghans who lived in the south, where the Taliban came to be based, endured much hardship from being associated with them.

The Taliban was not elected or chosen by the Afghan people. The Taliban first formed in the Peshawar region of Pakistan, which is near Afghanistan's southern border, and many believe that it was subservient to foreign networks that included Pakistan and Al Qaeda. Al Qaeda—composed mostly of Arabs, *not* Afghans—had gained a foothold in Afghanistan during the chaos of civil war, before the Taliban surfaced in the 1990s. Later the Taliban fed off the wealth of Osama bin Laden, and in return created a safe haven for bin Laden's terror-generating machine. So in effect, when the Taliban took control of the government, Afghanistan once again became the hostage of foreign forces.

If the Taliban really represented the Afghan people and were believed to be just and representative rulers, then Afghans would have joined them to resist the Western forces that bombed them in the months after September 11. Yet the Taliban were forced to move from one city to the other until their regime completely collapsed, at which point they had to flee to mountains and caves. Part of the reason that the West's war on terrorism has been successful in Afghanistan is that the people of Afghanistan did not resist them and in fact fought for the United States for the second time on the ground.

Initially, though, Afghanistan's people accepted the Taliban because they promised to bring stability to and restore a true Islamic nation. Prior to the Taliban, Afghanistan was lawless. Afghans needed a government, police, a constitution, courts, and authori-

---

[1] John C. Griffiths. *Afghanistan: A History of Conflict.* London: Carlton Books, 2001 (p. 230).

ties to appeal to when they were wronged. There was no recourse for people who were transgressed against. Criminals and warlords ran rampant, doing with the country and its people as they pleased. The Taliban fulfilled the people's basic need for safety and security.

During the chaotic, lawless times, many people claimed to have lost their wives and daughters to warlords or their agents through abduction. A family friend described how an entourage of men would appear before the home of a family who happened to have a pretty daughter. The men would ask for a sum of money that the family obviously would be unable to afford, then they took away the daughter as "payment." In many cases, they would rob the family and take the daughter anyway. Then, the daughter would be forcibly married to one of the men and used as a kind of slave to satisfy the husband's every whim. But these were the lucky ones, because many of these thugs would simply rape and murder their victims, discarding their bodies by the side of a river or mountain. As a result of this disgraceful practice, when an Afghan woman bore a daughter, she would feel cursed, because she knew the daughter would become a burden under these "law of the jungle" circumstances.

Then, in the mid-1990s, a group of young people who called themselves "the students," or Taliban, swept over Afghanistan. Other factions in the country gawked at how quickly they managed to take control of the country. Some believed that they were like a miracle, too good to be true. Some referred to them as soldiers of God who had come to rescue Afghanistan from its plight. Some also say that the Taliban had claimed to be representatives of the king in exile, Mohammed Zahir Shah, so that they could gain the people's initial and immediate support.

In any event, the Taliban did bring security to Afghanistan, but it was an extreme form of security, because the people were terrorized into subordination. If a person was convicted of doing wrong, he or she would be marched off to the soccer stadium, where an arm would be hacked off in plain view of the masses, to deter others who might even think of committing a crime. If adultery, murder, or any of the more serious crimes was charged, the accused was publicly executed.

The sad and unfortunate part is that this was all justified to the world under the banner of the religion of Islam. But Islam does not endorse these things, and nearly fourteen hundred years of history show that Muslims have not interpreted Islamic law in this manner. In fact, circumstances being what they were in Afghanistan, such punishments were simply un-Islamic.

For example, in Islamic law, cutting off an arm can be exercised only under extreme conditions. It is a maximum penalty for high crimes. But it is not independent of the government's role in fostering the behavior. In other words, a government cannot starve its people and then penalize them by cutting off their arms when they steal to feed themselves. There have been rare occasions when this law has actually been put into effect and exercised Islamically. It was not practiced in Afghanistan before the Taliban, although Afghanistan did have a system of capital punishment, as exists in America. But the Taliban made this into a regular event that was practiced quite casually. Between twenty years of war, land mines, and Taliban "justice," it makes one wonder what the country's future workforce will look like, with all its disfigured and dismembered people.

The Taliban's reactions and approaches were merciless by most standards. But Islam is a religion of mercy. Muslims are taught that if they have no mercy for people, then God will treat them with no mercy. Islam exhorts Muslims to temper justice with mercy. Although the Taliban's strict rule did serve its purpose in the sense that they managed to transform a wild and lawless country into a safe place in which one could leave a bundle of cash in the streets with no worries that anyone would dare take it, the price was too high for the Afghans to pay.

~≈ ≈~

The term *jihad* carries a great deal of social and political force, so much so that I am almost tempted to drop it from my vocabulary. But rather than do that, I think it better to fully explain this loaded word and try to understand its real meaning.

Jihad, or "holy war" as it has mistakenly come to be understood, is often conceived of as an Islamic license for killing those who are not of the Muslim faith. However, this could not be farther from the truth. Jihad actually refers to "struggle," and this struggle can take place on many levels, including social and spiritual. The Quran says, "Those who believe, and suffer exile and strive with might and main, in God's cause, with their goodness and their persons, have the highest rank in the sight of God. They are the people who will achieve salvation" (9:20). So the struggle to make ourselves better and improve upon the quality of our faith can be considered an inner jihad, whereas the struggle of resisting the threat to one's right to self-determination and defending territorial integrity is a jihad or struggle in the combative sense. The combative sense would encompass, for example, Afghans defending their country against the British colonizers of the nineteenth century or the Soviet invaders of the twentieth century. Muslims are not at all justified under Islam in killing innocent people of any faith to meet political agendas. The Quran says, "Fight in the cause of God those who fight you, but do not transgress limits; for God loveth not transgressors" (2:190).

The justification for jihad seems to hinge on how we define innocence. In Islamic terms, innocence is characterized in a time of war as those who are not engaged in the war at hand. According to Islamic law, women, children, male noncombatants (usually older men), and animal and plant life are all innocent entities that are not to be harmed during war.

Why is the killing of innocents happening, then, if it is so wrong, especially when these Muslims actually validate their practices with Islam? One answer lies with low-budget political organizations such as Al Qaeda—that is, low-budget relative to the governments they target. These organizations are not aimed at gaining approval from God as they claim, but at gaining real estate. Theirs is a very "this-worldly" cause. They are in the business of using terrorism to gain success. They do not have the financial capabilities to wage a real war against their enemy superpowers, so they recruit terrorists to carry out their plans. Certainly, the only way to convince these young, desperate souls to carry out these violent attacks is through offers of financial security for their families and assurances that they will go to heaven, as they will die for a true cause—that of Islam. Again, Muslims are extremely proud of their faith, whether they practice devoutly or not. To shroud one's political agendas with the cloak of Islam is to gain a great deal of support and sympathy for the cause in question from the rapidly growing Muslim population.

Proponents of acts of terror, particularly acts that result in suicide, believe that because they have such little ability to defend their rights, this is the only alternative left for striking back. Suicide is expressly forbidden in Islam, as it is in most other religions. But suicide attackers believe that what they are doing is just a combative strategy. They feel they must use themselves as missiles, since they quite simply cannot afford to get their hands on real ones.

The method of suicide attacks is very recent in Islamic history. Looking back in time, one doesn't find Muslims using themselves as weapons simply because the odds were against them. In fact, the most famous Islamic wars were successful despite seemingly impossible odds—as recently illustrated in Afghanistan. Muslims have relied on God Himself and have adhered to the Islamic code of conduct in war. Never did they take matters into their own hands. Despite the clear Islamic stance against it and the possibility of other creative ways to strike back at their enemies, suicide attackers choose to transgress the guidelines of war set forth by the Quran. It is a sadly desperate measure, and illustrates the huge need for East and West to start learning how to understand each other. Nonetheless, it is an un-Islamic measure by any interpretation.

Terrorism is defined by philosopher Andrew Valls as the destruction of people or property for political reasons. This is prohibited in Islam. This definition allows that politically motivated destruction can be carried out on a state-sponsored level, which is then given the label of war, or on an individual or organizational level, which is then referred to as terrorism—though it is the same physical act that is carried out.

The most common forms of terrorism, and the most recent kind, which was demonstrated in the September 11 attacks, target innocent civilians in order to express a disgruntled and unheard opinion about foreign policy. This is *not* an Islamic practice. In declaring war, it is not ethically acceptable to destroy that which is unrelated to the elimination of the actual danger to oneself. Innocent people who have no influence or decision-making ability with regard to policies that pose a threat and who have not engaged in the war itself are not justifiable targets of war. The fact that the citizens of democratic nations vote their leaders into government, thereby giving those leaders the authority to continue their policies, is used as justification by some terrorist organizations to target civilians. But that logic doesn't work in the realm of Islamic warfare and principles, and also displays gross cowardice.

I realize that this characterization of Islam is quite different from how some like to portray it. Some want to justify the violence in the Middle East as part of Muhammad's (pbuh) command to spread Islam through the sword. Granted, all of world history reflects bloodshed, and the Middle East is no exception. But sometimes I wonder where these wild myths and misconceptions about Islam started, when they are not embedded in its rhetoric nor its philosophy, and how they have taken hold in the minds of people for so long.

The week after the attacks on America, I was told by a friend that his Sunday sermon at church informed him that terrorists engage in this behavior because the Quran promises them seventy-two virgin women and eternal bliss in paradise as a reward for their acts of terrorism. These are fairy tales that are based on a misinterpretation of Islamic doctrine; in fact, the whole issue of these "virgins" might be a mirage, according to a recent analysis that delves into such obscurities in the Quran.[2] Such misinterpretations give Islam a barbaric image and further tarnish the remnants of understanding between the East and the West. As is clearly illustrated by the Quran, harm to innocent life and suicide are simply wrong in Islam, just as wrong as in any other monotheistic religion of the Abrahamic tradition.

Islam does *not* teach that killing a Jew or Christian will guarantee one's place in heaven. The Quran relates:

> Those who believe (in the Quran) and those who follow the Jewish (scriptures), and the Christians and the Sabians, and who believe in God and the last day, and work righteousness, shall have their reward there from twelve springs. Each group knew its own place for water [referring to the twelve tribes of Israel, from the sons of Jacob]. So eat and drink of the sustenance provided by God, and do no evil nor mischief on the face of the earth. (2:62)

Despite popular belief, Christians and Jews are not even considered to be unbelievers or pagans. They are referred to in the Quran as the "people of the book," because they abide by one of the four books that are accepted in Islam as being the authentic revelations of God: the Bible, Psalms, Torah, and finally the Quran. Muslims share the same prophets as Christians and Jews. "Unbelievers" applies only to those who do not recognize the exis-

---

[2]The British newspaper *The Guardian* ran an article addressing a study that suggests that a proper translation shows that the so-called "virgins" in question are actually "white raisins"—in other words, those who go to heaven will be rewarded with food and drink, not women. See Ibn Warraq, "Virgins? What Virgins?" (January 12, 2002).

tence of their creator, and "pagans" are those who worship man-made, manufactured idols.

However, some ignorant and uneducated Muslims reinforce the ridiculous claims that are made on their religion, and inject hatred into their pseudo-education system. It was this kind of pseudo-education that produced the Taliban in the *madrasas*, or schools, in Pakistan. The Taliban carried out what they knew to be true; however, they were trained to hate, not to tolerate and embrace, as Islam teaches Muslims to do.

The Taliban's merciless punishments and killings of people who are suspected of crimes cannot be construed as Islamic. A verse in the Quran describes how God tells the Prophet Muhammad (pbuh) that He has sent him for no other reason than as a mercy to mankind. The Taliban, who claimed to uphold Islam, practiced no mercy on those they ruled, and therefore counteracted the purpose of God's intentions in sending the Prophet Muhammad (pbuh) to mankind. The Taliban cannot be said to represent Islam any more than the Inquisition, pedophiliac priests, or David Koresh can be said to represent Christianity. The followers of a religion are not the religion itself. Certainly, Islam existed well before the Taliban and will continue to flourish after them.

Furthermore, Middle Eastern culture is not the same thing as the religion of Islam. Middle Eastern culture is a conservative system of values based on the ideals of an ancient civilization. These cultural values often clash with the broad-minded values found in Islam. When Islam originally was born in Arabia, it was a revolutionary doctrine that modernized the Arabs out of their ignorance (*jahiliya* in Arabic). Before Islam, Arabs often buried their newborn daughters alive. They married a limitless number of women and bought, sold, or traded them as commodities. Islam replaced these cultural practices with universal religious ones that were meant for all times and all peoples.

Unfortunately, Middle Eastern cultural practices are generalized and projected by many onto the religion of Islam, so if an atrocity or human rights violation is committed in the Middle East, it is seen as a Muslim thing. To conceive of Middle Eastern culture as the same as Islam is a huge fallacy that leads to discrimination and erroneous profiling of an enormously diverse group of individuals.

We are making an enemy out of a world population of a billion Muslims rather than confronting the real culprits. In fact, despite the tragic events of recent years, Islam continues to be the world's fastest-growing religion. It is more likely that the religion is growing because of its overarching positive doctrines and not its hate-based, fringe mutations.

~≈ ≈~

Before the awakening of my religious consciousness, I was a Muslim, but only by name. I called myself a Muslim and was quite vehement about the solidity of that, when in reality my assertion was a façade. The actions and behaviors that I engaged in then might be considered un-Islamic, and yet I was a Muslim. For that matter, even now that I am conscious of my religious values, I certainly make mistakes, whether I acknowledge them or not. I am not some kind of infallible, walking Quran. People are not perfect. We seem to understand this and acknowledge it in most people, but somehow Muslims seem to be held to a different standard.

I practice the tenets of Islam more than before, but I don't claim to single-handedly uphold and represent the religion of Islam, and neither can anyone else. The only living example of Islam was the Prophet Muhammad (pbuh), as well as the other messengers of God or prophets, who included Adam, Moses, Jesus, David, Noah, Jacob, Joseph, and others (peace be upon them).

In fact, it was this kind of social pressure that led me to take off my hijab after high school. I felt that any move I made, and every word I uttered, was considered by both Muslims and non-Muslims alike as the "voice of Islam." Without being an Islamic scholar or perfect by any standard, this was too heavy a burden to bear.

Why did everyone think that wearing a head scarf somehow made me a living representation of Islam? I also noticed that Muslim men who wore beards were seen as scholars or true representatives of Islam, when in fact they were just a bunch of average guys.

In contemporary times, we find men in the world who not only claim to represent the religion of Islam but profess to safeguard the authentic and sacred context of the religion within their country's governmental policies. One example is the Taliban, who claimed that they were enforcing true Islamic laws in Afghanistan when in fact the Prophet Muhammad (pbuh) never beat women nor banned them from school. In regard to stealing, Islam requires the state to play its part in society and share the blame when people are forced to desperate measures, and the maximum penalty for crimes cannot be exercised as a result. In regard to education, Muhammad (pbuh) stated that Muslims should go as far as China to attain knowledge. The system of mathematics based on Arabic numerals at the beginning of the Islamic civilization contributed greatly to various disciplines the world over. Muslims also instituted the works of the great philosopher Aristotle, which might have been lost otherwise. Banning anyone from receiving an education goes against the basis of Islamic civilization.

I understand why the non-Muslim community might be quick to jump to the conclusion that a man who wears a certain style of beard or a woman who wears a head scarf must know what they are talking about regarding Islam. After all, if you do not know about Islam, and Muslims who should know about it say that they do, then you conclude that they must. This is the exact mentality that has allowed oppressive dictatorships to take hold in the Middle East. The people of the Middle East are immersed in a great deal of ignorance as a result of the high illiteracy rate. Most Afghans, who don't speak Arabic, are clueless as to the meaning of the Quran. Even my parents' generation learned to read the Quran but were never taught the meaning.

Afghans often relied on local mullahs to learn about Islam. The

Middle East has become infamous for its corrupt mullahs who have skewed and molded the meaning of Islam to conform to their own agendas, needs, and desires. Sometimes mullahs might have had good intentions; for instance, a mullah who wanted his community to unite or to believe more deeply might invent a story, designed to bind people together, that supposedly came from the Prophet Muhammad (pbuh) or the Quran. The problem was that these mullahs were usually uneducated, and so their stories, which were often quite animated, were reduced to absurdity. This counteracted their effectiveness, as people who listened to these stories might have grown to think of Islam as a feeble doctrine, whether they openly admitted it or not.

Millions of Afghans who were and continue to be illiterate are not able to understand or read a translation of the Quran. These people are totally vulnerable to what their leaders and mullahs tell them. These have often been men who are not qualified to be in a position of leadership and who strong-arm their way into power by claiming to know the truth of Islam and telling people what to believe. In this way, Afghans, as well as other people throughout the East, have been used and abused by their own leaders who are willing to capitalize on their followers' faith and trust. It is imperative that Afghans and all Muslims throughout the world seek a truer understanding of their religion through direct dialogue and interaction rather than relying on second-hand commentators, who invariably offer them artificial views that are politically or culturally motivated.

Afghans are proud of their faith in Islam. They have a hard time agreeing on much, but it is easy to gain convergence of opinion when it comes to the will of Allah.[3] If Afghans find themselves without the necessities to live, they simply accept their circumstances as ordained by the will of God. Many Muslims who live

---

[3]*Allah* is the Arabic word for God, just as *Dios* is the Spanish word and *Dieu* is the French word. Christian and Jewish Arabs all call their god Allah. Thus, Allah is not a separate entity from the monotheistic God.

in Afghanistan cannot pride themselves on anything else but their Islamic faith, courage, bravery, and honor. This is all they have left at this point in history, but it has proved to be enough for them to survive.

During the U.S. air strikes in Afghanistan in 2001, I saw a group of Afghan people who had been relocated from their bomb-riddled village to an area that looked like it came out of a biblical scene. All that could be seen for miles was the brown dirt of the ground and a beautiful blue sky above. People in typical Afghan garb rode on their donkeys to their new settlement. One woman was sharing her feelings of hopelessness because there was no food or water to be found anywhere. Then another gentleman spoke up in a strong-willed fashion. He said that it must have been meant for him and his people to be in that barren location, so they must accept God's will and their fate with full belief and confidence that it was not something meaningless, coincidental, or senseless. I supposed that their faith would be the only thing that could maintain their sanity in the midst of watching their entire civilization perish before their eyes.

Islam is not a religion of hate, a religion that teaches killing in exchange for seventy-two virgins, a religion that approves of killing innocent life, or a religion that condones suicide. It is a religion of peace, as are all of the great monotheistic religions, as are many other religions as well. Connecting Islam with these negative stereotypes is as bad as connecting *all* Christianity with hatred of infidels, connecting *all* Jews with greed and self-interest, and connecting those who follow no particular religion with loose lives of indulgence in alcohol and sex. The few never represent all. We must distinguish between the followers of a religion and the religion itself. Corrupt people will always afflict our world, and the ugly face of terrorism and hate is bound by no religion or race. If we blanket entire groups with our stereotypes of a few, then we leave no room for understanding, mutual exchange, or peaceful coexistence.

Islamic history attests to the fact that the true Islamic state is merciful and can provide a healthy society. Afghanistan is a Muslim nation that has an opportunity to realize the democratic, just, religiously tolerant, and peaceful ways of the true Islamic state. It seems that in the face of so much diversity, Islam, whose beliefs are shared across ethnic lines, could prove to be the binding ingredient that will glue together a divided nation.

Islam is a way of life and must be understood properly both by its followers and others. Hopefully, the United States' relationship with Afghanistan, which began to take shape again only after the events of September 11, will prove to be a lasting and harmonious one. In the future, when the U.S. finds itself in relationships (good or bad) with other Muslim countries, we should keep in mind that the principles that those countries operate under are similar to Afghanistan's—and in many cases are even more exaggerated. Our old and new experiences with Afghanistan will be a paradigm for how we interact with the entire Muslim world.

⁓ Eight ⁓

Between Old Friends

I t is a point of pride for Afghans that their poor, behind-the-times country defeated the British invaders in the nineteenth century and the Soviet ones in the twentieth. In the twenty-first century, the Taliban hoped to harness this pride to rally Afghans against yet another attacking superpower, the United States. But the Taliban's plan didn't work, because the Afghan people didn't view the U.S. as their enemy.

Glued to television news after the September 11 catastrophe, I noticed that Afghans who were being interviewed in Afghanistan had no need for a translator. How do these people, who have had no access to schools or other academic resources for years, know how to speak English? It comes from the Afghans' love affair with the West and with America in particular. When my parents were college students in the 1970s, they and their peers dressed according to what was stylish in the West. Guys wore their hair in Beatles-style cuts and girls wore theirs stringy and bone-straight. Bellbottom pants and platform shoes were a common sight. Even under the Taliban, which had strict rules about haircuts, the style sported by Leonardo DiCaprio in the film *Titanic* was immensely popular and provided by barbers who were willing to break the rules.

Afghan singers imitated American music. The superstar singer of Afghanistan, the late Ahmad Zahir, sang Farsi versions of El-vis's tunes and added a Western twist to traditional Afghan music. Afghan youth enjoyed reading journals and magazines from neigh-boring Iran, which were often based on Western novels and mur-der mysteries. They delved into romance novels that seemed to be taken right out of American ones and translated into Farsi. Even the initial willingness of some Afghans to embrace a foreign gov-ernment power like the Soviet Union signified Afghanistan's de-sire to become more like a Western state.

Many Afghans have told me that America is seen as a kind of oasis, the ideal place to get a prestigious education and settle down to a life of opportunity. With most jobs in Afghanistan being in government ministries, the military, or education, there wasn't much opportunity for aspiring college graduates who wanted something more out of life. My paternal grandmother, Koh Koh Jan, told me of her aspirations to make it to the United States one day, the lush green land of the free, an advanced country with glass sidewalks where everyone was wealthy. She said that every person she knew in Afghanistan aspired to the lofty dream of being able to visit America one day, but few dared to treat it as more than a fantasy.

But more important than offering its culture and educational and economic opportunities, the U.S. helped Afghanistan defeat the Soviet invaders. A few years after the Soviets invaded, the U.S. began providing Afghan resistance forces with various forms of relief. This made Afghans feel that the U.S., especially the Reagan administration (which gave the mujahideen their most ef-fective weapon — Stinger missiles), was a true and loyal friend. They thought that the U.S. had a genuine interest in their country and wanted to help them defend their autonomy.

Afghans liked to think that the U.S. noticed their bravery, cour-age, loyalty, and character. They believed they were working side by side to help defeat the Red Army — though the Afghans were the ones actually fighting the war, while the U.S. supplied them with the money, training, and weapons they needed to do it. As one American said, "It was our goal, and it was their blood." But Americans did not need to fight physically as they had in Vietnam, because Afghans were able to carry out the fight on their own.

It had always seemed to me that the strong ability of Afghans to fight in wars was something that came naturally to them, without effort. I took it for granted that Afghans who lived in Afghanistan would defend the country, come what may—historically they had never tasted defeat. This was an easy attitude for me to take, sitting in my comfortable home in Southern California, patiently waiting for the Afghans to win so that one day the country would be safe for me and my Afghan-American compatriots to visit again. I didn't think much about who was paying the price for this luxury I had.

My conversations with an older man from the mosque I attend put things into perspective for me. I still do not know his name; I address him simply as "Uncle," because it would be rude to ask an elder his first name. I met Uncle in the month of Ramadan. I had slipped into the mosque between the scheduled prayer times, when no one else was there, and began to pray alone, with full concentration. Apparently, I was not all alone, as this older gentleman who looked like my grandfather was there watching what I was doing.

When I came out of the prayer room, he greeted me with a package of dates from Saudi Arabia. He wore a long rough beard with a turban, traditional Afghan dress, and a white shawl over his shoulders. He surely had drawn stares as he walked to the mosque from his home. He asked me in English who I was. When he found out I was Afghan, his eyes lit up—he had presumed I was Arab. He too was Pashtun, which became evident to me by his heavy accent when he spoke in Farsi, by the way he referred to himself in the plural *("Ma . . .")*, and the way he replaced all of the *p* sounds in words with *f*. He was intent on having me marry any one of his eight sons, and asked me to take my pick!

He then told me that he had been a fighter and leader in the Soviet war. I was surprised, as he seemed so old, but his mind and heart were vigorously young. When I asked him about his experiences there, he began to tell me of the weighty load that was on the shoulders of the Afghans. He said that they were fighting with a power that they could not compete with on any level except ideology. "We believed in God, and they believed in nothing," he said. "There was no comparison in that arena."

My charismatic new uncle's large eyes grew even larger when he told me stories of his time in combat. Once his leg was injured and he thought for sure that he would die, but he was saved by another young man who literally would not let him go. This young man had grown quite attached to him throughout their experiences, and opened up to him about his life. He was engaged to be married and had many reasons to want to live, but those reasons did not outweigh what his soul could not let go of, his beloved Afghanistan. He said that he had many opportunities to flee the country to safety but would never be able to, even though it made perfect sense to get out—only a senseless person would stay, waiting to be wiped out. And in fact, before the two of them made it back to safety, the young man shielded Uncle from gunfire and absorbed a hit, dying immediately.

Uncle said that the Afghan fighters thought that all of their blood and sacrifice would eventually turn out to be the price for Afghanistan's freedom. But then Uncle's face grew dim. He said that when the war ended, the Afghans were struck with some harsh realities. They had not negotiated any kind of accord with the United States for postwar reconstruction. Such a thing would not even have crossed their minds, as their friendship with their American ally presumably took care of everything. Obviously, when you are a friend, you do everything in your power to help your friend in troubled times. No one expects you to turn your back and leave after you get what you want; this would not be friendship. Rather, it would be taking advantage of the trusting nature of earnest people. And it wasn't as though the U.S. couldn't afford it, or that they did not give aid to other countries. So, he said, the Afghans were surprised when America made no gesture to help the war-torn country after its political Cold War goals were met there.

A little more than a decade after the Soviet withdrawal, the United States has finally returned to Afghanistan. The reason was to apprehend bin Laden and his Al Qaeda network. This evolved into an interest in removing the Taliban, which not only harbored terrorists suspected of hurting the U.S. but also caused a great deal of pain for the Afghan people. But some Afghans were skeptical about why the U.S. was removing the Taliban now, since they had been committing human rights atrocities years prior to this recent spurt of awareness.

For years, the U.S. made virtually no contact with the people of Afghanistan. One excuse was that the Taliban had destroyed radios and other forms of mass communication. Even during the U.S. air strikes on Afghanistan, the Afghans didn't understand why America was bombing their country to even more ruination than before. They could only hold on to their suspicion that it was because the U.S. hated the Taliban. Finally they realized that bin Laden was the target, but why he was a target remained a mystery to many who did not even know about the September 11 attacks.

Though we in the U.S. were informed of the care that was taken to avoid civilian casualties, Afghans were not aware of these attempts or intentions. I heard of many Afghans who were appalled that they were being made to pay for bin Laden when they felt certain that he had escaped safely in the first weeks after the September 11 attacks, prior to the commencement of the air strikes. I watched one older Afghan man on television who spent his days during the U.S. attacks retrieving dead children from the ground. He pointed to fragments of U.S.-made bombs and angrily screamed at the reporter, "You say America is trying to help and liberate us. Look at our dead children! Is this how they plan on helping us?" He angrily threw the pieces of the bombs away.

Afghans were confused about why the U.S. was at war with their country. They had no media or other avenues of communication that could tell them of the atrocities in New York, Washington, and Pennsylvania. Their country had crumbled into ruins, to the point that they thought it could not possibly get any worse, and yet it did. One Afghan who was interviewed by a television reporter naively asked, "Why are they bombing us in the first place, and then dumping food packets on us like we were a pack of dogs?"

I watched on the news as a Western journalist took copies of an American news magazine that had photos of the burning World Trade Center towers to Afghanistan to try to explain to them what had sparked the bombings of their country. The people flocked around him. They were dumbfounded at the series of events that the journalist said had transpired.

Afghans had suspected that the Taliban and bin Laden had somehow gotten into a political collision with the United States. Yet they were confused about why the Taliban and bin Laden were not being annihilated or captured personally. Many Afghans believed bin Laden must have escaped Afghanistan before the U.S. bombing campaign even began, because they felt that he would not possibly wait for the U.S. to come and catch him. Moreover, they believe the power and expertise of the U.S. to be so great that "accidents," such as the escapes of Mullah Omar and bin Laden, or the deaths of Afghan civilians, could not be accidents at all. The U.S. is admired for its might, but its might precludes any justification for failure; therefore, its actions are seen as calculated and deliberate and are subject to great scrutiny.

Many Afghans, both living in Afghanistan and those abroad, feel that the level of bombing that occurred there was more comprehensive than surgical. It seemed to them that the goal was to level the country in hopes of hitting bin Laden in the sweep. Others feel that the air strikes were a way for the American people to blow off retaliatory steam, by "bombing Afghanistan back to the Stone Age." Of course, it wasn't simple retaliation; Afghanistan had nothing to do with the attacks on America, but rather happened to be the country chosen by bin Laden to hide in.

Afghans are well aware that bin Laden was trained by the CIA, and are at a loss as to why they have to pay for an American-supported and American-trained ally gone bad. What did they do to deserve this pandemonium? A foreign network led by a non-Afghan decided to move into their country and dupe its government into submission and subservience. The leaders of this regime and bin Laden remain at large, while Afghans died to pay the price for them—some swiftly, some painfully and slowly. The U.S. may not have intended this result, but the concrete events that unfolded feed some suspicions that the U.S. has more nefarious motives.

Following the attacks in 2001, there has been a strong American presence in Afghanistan. While Afghans generally welcome the United States' help in peacekeeping as well as its leadership in pushing Afghans to come to the table to hash out a new government, some fear that it might intervene too deeply and inappropriately in Afghan government, stripping the Afghans of their true sovereignty and ability to preside over their own affairs without intervention—things that have eluded them for far too long.

After all their tough experiences, the Afghans have lost their naivete and now speculate about the international community's continued involvement in their lost civilization. Many possible reasons are floating about for America's interest in Afghanistan after all those years of silence. Now, some Afghans say that the future oil pipeline project and the amount of gas that has been discovered in Afghanistan is the key interest, while others emphasize the strategic geographical location of the country, which would make it a military jewel for the United States. Some point to the fact that the U.S. wants an ally in the region to widen its sphere of influence. Others argue that the September 11 attacks will be used by the U.S. as a license to go into any country of its choice, whether in peace or in war, so it can either eradicate their military or impose any intended Western goal. The now-skeptical Afghans contend that it wouldn't be the first time that a foreign power that had claimed to be friend ousted the existing rulers, set up a puppet regime, and enforced its values upon the people.

❧ ❧

In America, we mourn the loss of the victims of September 11: those who died in the World Trade Center, those who died at the Pentagon, and those who were on the planes that were destroyed, as well as those who have lost their lives in the subsequent war on terrorism. We even mourn the loss of the twin towers themselves as a symbol of life and freedom.

However, the subsequent U.S. air strikes on Afghanistan led to "Afghan victims of 9/11." Afghanistan paid a heavy price for the attacks of September 11. The lush landscape, greenery, sweet air, and beautiful people of Afghanistan have been ravaged by a variety of foreign forces. Afghan parents feel the loss of their children as keenly as the parents of victims of September 11. They search through rubble and dirt to find their children, their only hope in life, so that they might at least honor them with a proper burial. And death is not the only thing that devastates. Afghanistan's landmarks are timeless and priceless. The people of Afghanistan hold their country's architectural and artistic heritage in high esteem; it is not just the beauty of their art that creates pride, but the fact that they are touchstones for their society. No restoration would come close to compensating for the loss of their original state.

Two deeply wounded nations are now letting their grief turn into feelings of suspicion, betrayal, and mistrust — at a time when we need each other the most. There must be a bridge that can span the huge gap between Afghanistan and the United States.

Now that it is possible to visit Afghanistan freely, I find myself experiencing a heightened awareness of my connection to my roots in Afghanistan. Yet in some ways I feel an even more heightened sense of connection to the United States now, as do many other Afghans who have suddenly shifted from refugee to true immigrant status. In other words, now they actually have a choice—to go back or to stay here.

The Afghanistan that I knew as a child has been transformed on all levels into a place that hardly resembles it. Though I feel obligated to give back to that society what I have learned and gained from the U.S.—the skills that so many Afghan women need—I fear a culture shock and perhaps even culture clash. Though I am willing to adhere to the cultural norms in Afghanistan, I am not certain of the reception Afghan-Americans will receive or whether we will be viewed as outsiders altogether. Afghan-Americans must anticipate that Afghans might feel some resentment, or at least feel that we are outsiders and not authentic on some level because they have always fought and lived within the country. But this is only one small facet of the realities that Afghan-Americans will face in returning to Afghanistan.

I shudder at the thought of the extent of psychological trauma that the women and children have suffered as a result of the wars. I am almost afraid to go back, to have to face those realities directly rather than hear about them from a distance. I wonder, will the beautiful cherry orchards and crystal streams of Paghman still be there? What about my grandparents' home, where I met them for the first and last time—will that too be destroyed? I dread finding out the answers to these and an endless number of other questions.

Yet I do hope to participate in restoring Afghanistan by assisting in the opening of girls' schools. For the last few years Afghan girls have been unfairly deprived of education, an opportunity that I have had the luxury of fully pursuing in America. It is now my duty to enter a new dimension of activism by helping the young women of Afghanistan rediscover this endlessly rewarding realm of experience. Perhaps working with Afghan girls in the schools and universities will help bring some meaning to the destruction incurred by both Afghanistan in the last few decades and the United States on September 11, 2001.

When I first became involved in community activism, I wondered what a divided, bicultural Afghan-American, who found it so hard to fit into both Afghan and American circles, really could do to help matters in the West or East. For most of my life I believed that not being able to fully socialize into either community was a horrible fate that left me with an alien identity and made me a member of nowhere. I didn't think about the possibility that it might make me a member of both cultures. In the case of bridging the gap between Afghanistan and America, I now believe that my divided identity has the potential to finally achieve a greater meaning and purpose. By this I mean to say that the bridge between Afghanistan and America *is* Afghan-Americans.

Afghan-Americans are key to bringing together these disparate societies. Our unique ability to see both sides of the coin is the real beauty of the hyphenated Afghan. We can help unite our communities by acting as a point of reference that is not blind to the concerns of either side. Now that Afghan-Americans are feeling a commitment to return to Afghanistan to contribute to its rebuilding, we should realize that we are in a wonderful position to help mend the lost relationship between Afghanistan and the U.S., since we are the ones best equipped to do it. We are also in a position to further mutual understanding by explaining the value systems and ideologies of both countries.

Of course, all kinds of people will be going to Afghanistan in the rebuilding efforts. Foreign enterprises will come to develop infrastructure, build homes, set up schools, invest in businesses, dispense humanitarian aid, and consult on government affairs. These people will have technical expertise, but they will not necessarily know how to share the positive cultural values that America has to offer without imposing them or creating friction with the people they are trying to help. Brokering a new relationship between

Afghans and Westerners will be a very delicate matter. Judicious Afghan-Americans will be able to help determine what cultural norms are compatible with the society. We have gained a keen insight on how to create a credible synthesis between the two, as we have been doing within the microcosms of our own lives.

Doctors, engineers, entrepreneurs, teachers, and people from all walks of life with knowledge or skills to offer are on a mission to go back to Afghanistan and play a part in the reconstruction efforts. Some are still skeptical about the safety and security of the country and continue to wait for a sign that the dust has settled. Others are simply diving in headfirst, eager to get moving on their newfound purpose. Some friends who left for Afghanistan in the weeks after September 11 have already gained high-ranking positions in the country's government. They share an optimistic view of the future of Afghanistan and encourage more Afghans to return.

I anticipate that Afghan-Americans will be rejuvenated with a new sense of pride that will stem both from aiding their fellow Afghans and seeing their homeland rebuilt by the hands of the Afghans themselves. This priceless reward will undoubtedly help fill the vacuum of identity gaps and sense of personhood that was lost in the dynamic of forming the Afghan-American persona.

Some Afghan-Americans might choose to stay in Afghanistan, while others will decide to return to the U.S. The fact that there is now a choice of whether to stay or go adds a great sense of empowerment that did not exist before. When friends of mine would talk about spending their summer vacations in their native countries of Lebanon or Israel, I wished I could say the same of Afghanistan, where no one was allowed to enter or leave. As they talked about the improvements that were taking place in their home countries, I could only think about how mine was deteriorating into ruin. A sense of normalcy in Afghanistan has brought life back to the Afghan community abroad and a resurgence of energy that has lifted spirits immeasurably.

My parents have a bittersweet view about going back. They know that they will not be returning to the same country they left. My dad says he would like to use his pharmaceutical experience to help Afghans gain access to vitamins, medication, and vaccines that are manufactured locally. My mom would like to volunteer to teach at the girls' schools to pay back her debt for the college education she received at the expense of Kabul University and was never able to put to use there. However, she feels sad going back now when her parents have passed away.

There is an entire generation of Afghans who were born abroad and have yet to see Afghanistan for the first time. This new crop talks about how excited they are to "change things around" over there so that no more tragedies befall the country. They have the typical attitude of all young people—that they have all the solutions and need to come to the country's rescue—and I do not doubt that they will put their heart and soul into their work.

Will these Afghan-Americans who go to Afghanistan and then return to the United States help educate Americans about the realities of Afghans and Afghanistan? I get a certain sense of pleasure from watching President Hamid Karzai win praise throughout the West for his bold fashion statements in Afghan garb—a small step, to be sure, but an important one that reflects the ability of Americans to respect and admire a foreign culture. I wonder if we can renew the Afghan people's admiration for America, so that the feeling can be sincerely mutual once again.

As the United States and Afghanistan begin a fresh relationship, dialogue will be essential to its success. This dialogue cannot be mediated by secondhand commentators who claim to know what Afghans, Muslims, or Americans believe. Rather, we must be willing to listen to people directly, with open hearts and minds. Instead of giving all our attention to those who cloud the picture by giving us their artificial views, we must lend our ears to the actual people whom we want to know.

~❦ *Nine* ❦~

As the Smoke Clears

The day that marked a pivotal change in the world order arrived gently, with no warning or clue that it would be any different from any other. The sun was warm and bright, much as it was on that day in Kabul when I first saw a tank and Afghanistan changed forever.

I was sleeping in, as I usually stay awake studying until late in the evening. Tucked away in bed, I received a call that I almost did not answer. When I finally picked up the phone, I heard a relative frantically telling me to turn on the news. I jumped out of bed and turned on the television to a surreal scene of the two tall trade towers, one with a hole in it and smoke rising from it. The voice of the news reporter kept echoing in my ears as he said the words I cannot forget: "America is under attack! I repeat, America is under attack—and we do not know who the enemy is!" Soon the second tower was hit, then the Pentagon, and then a plane went down in a Pennsylvania field.

Living in Los Angeles, I was scared that we might be next. I tried to make sure that the family, especially my brother and sister, were safe and secure, and then proceeded to stay glued to the television for days, which turned into months. We were all devastated by what had transpired with such ease and no warning, yet the magnitude of the situation was so penetrating that it took months for the full reality to settle in. *What had happened? How could this have happened?* Speculation began to race that the attacks had been committed by bin Laden, who was taking shelter in Afghanistan. I realized then that this was not the end of the tragedy but only the beginning. I cringed to think of the atrocities that were yet to come. When the U.S. decided to bomb Afghanistan, I found myself torn in two.

There is a clear dividing line in my life: before September 11 and after it. Before, there was little or no public knowledge of Afghanistan, its cultural practices, religious persuasion, or even geographical location. Whenever I was asked what my national heritage was, my reply of Afghanistan would have to be followed with some descriptive highlights and an explanation of where it was on the map. Such an introduction is no longer necessary; now even the most sheltered people can rattle off names such as Tora Bora and Kandahar. However, it is their perception of the country that is troublesome.

I don't think people really know how to react toward Afghans and especially Muslims. On one hand, President Bush has made a clear distinction between the people of Afghanistan, whom the U.S. liberated from Taliban control, and the Al Qaeda network affiliated with Osama bin Laden. It is a known fact that none of the terrorists directly involved with the attacks of September 11 were Afghan. Bush has also made it clear that the religion of Islam is a religion of peace. On the other hand, the media shows us piteous images of poor women and children enduring horrible trials, yet in the same breath tells us of their deep hatred for our country and their support of bin Laden.

I continue to see images of Afghans in the media being implicitly portrayed as savage animals. One newspaper article that surfaced in 2001 showed a beautiful young Afghan woman at the beauty salon preparing for her wedding. Though it should have been a happy time for her, the reporter said, she was sad because her mother was not present: Her father had stabbed her to death with a pair of scissors for not keeping the baby quiet. I don't doubt the truth of the story. It's the context—at a time when Americans are just getting to know the Afghan people—that I find questionable. I feel the media has been responsible in part for much of the skewed information we receive. Certainly, as Walter Kronkite has stated, if America is relying on the current media as their source of world news, then they are at a loss.

Since I was a teenager I have been actively monitoring the media, which seems to commit the gravest sin in how they portray Muslims and Middle Eastern people. I invariably see images that reinforce stereotypes, such as women draped in burqas walking three feet behind their husbands or savage men indulging in belly dancers and harems. The sad part is that these images are coupled with the Muslim call to prayer and depictions of Muslims praying. This connection is monumentally wrong. It sends the message that pious Muslims practice such evil deeds, when in fact Islam stands for the opposite.

There seems to be almost no effort to balance these images with those of the actual personalities and characters inside the homes of families. When a personal look is attempted, it usually involves women who are being abused, or an American woman married to a Middle Eastern man who kidnapped their children. It is similar to how American women are portrayed in the Middle East: as degraded by American men and perceived only as sex objects. Though that takes place, it certainly cannot be viewed as typical of American women.

The general impression that the media gives is that Afghan men as well as all Muslim men are barbaric toward women. The characteristics of the Taliban are generalized to all Afghan men, and Afghan women are depicted as brainwashed into submission. While such cases exist, they are not the norm for Afghans, and I am disappointed to see the Afghans perceived so negatively.

Afghan women have proven their strong will and determination even in the face of impossible struggles. They have maintained their families and have continued their education in hiding. They have resisted the oppression of the Taliban. The choice of some of them to adopt their cultural burqa dress does not mean that they are robotically following the Taliban's demands. But they are *Afghan*, and abide by a different set of cultural norms than Americans.

I have come to realize that if we rely on the media as our only source of information, we will be utterly misguided. It is clear to me that we must treat with skepticism the things we hear or read about. We must either become critical thinkers who question authority or continue living in ignorance.

In 1991, when I was in high school, Iraq was regarded as the enemy and a source of evil. Today, because the war on terrorism focuses on no specific country, the enemy has been widened to include the entire Muslim world; Afghanistan, which contained many of the camps that trained these international killers, is at the heart of the conflict. As the native Afghan language of Pashto is transformed into the language of the Taliban enemy, and my grandfather's hometown of Kandahar becomes the foes' stronghold, I find myself in an awkward position as someone who cherishes my Afghan heritage and yet appreciates the myriad blessings of living in America.

I am in the position of having to justify my loyalty to America, which has now suddenly come into question. If I share any critical views of our government or foreign policy, they are no longer viewed as simply politically incorrect, leftist, or overly conservative, but as unpatriotic, insulting, and perhaps even criminal. My very presence arouses suspicion as to whose side I am really on, as if I am a kind of sleeper agent who will eventually show my true colors. I feel it in the reactions I get from people when I speak, and in the questions they ask me as they try to probe my mind about what's "really" going on in the world. One woman recently asked me about my nationality; when I told her my heritage was Afghan, she said, "So, do you anticipate any other terrorist attacks anytime soon?" How would I possibly know what bin Laden or any other terrorist plans on doing any more than other American citizens? But to calm her, I said I had a feeling that this would be it for a while.

Immediately after September 11, I went to see a professor to discuss a proposal for a paper that I wanted to present for class. He ended up talking to me for more than an hour about my Afghan roots and my political views. The professor told me that when he had told his wife that he had a student from Afghanistan, she said to him, "Oh, no! They're going to blow up USC!" He was candid with me about the feelings that were circulating, and though it was disappointing, I appreciated the reality check he gave me on my new position in American society.

When I go to the mosque for Friday prayer or any other religious event, I am always conscious of the danger involved as a result of the outbreak of anti-Islamic sentiment. Security guards have been hired to protect us as we pray to God. After the plot to bomb the King Fahd mosque in Culver City, California—a mosque that my family regularly attends—I wonder if Muslims will ever feel at home here again. I have taken to reading more about the experiences of the Japanese during World War II. I feel that Muslims are experiencing something similar in this country. Of course, we are not being shipped off to internment camps, but the discrimination we feel is very real.

I hope for a renewed sense of the place and role of Muslims and Middle Eastern people in American society. As the media plays a large role in shaping our views and perspectives, I would love it if shows such as Barbara Walters' "The View," a thoughtful and racially balanced television program designed to relate a variety of perspectives, had a Muslim woman on to add her voice to its diverse perspectives. It is through open dialogue that we can gain understanding and overcome the fears and hostilities we harbor. As we read books in school about the struggles of African-American and Hispanic people in this country, we should include this other predominant American minority in the dialogue.

⇜ ⇝

I truly adore the academic life — even more so now because intellectuals on the whole seem to be less susceptible to the plague of ignorance. Although I have faced hostility after September 11, I have also been asked to speak at conferences and share my thoughts on post-September 11 events. My words are absorbed by the audience and treated as almost prophetic. There is more interest in my background and my views.

I teach a course on contemporary ethical issues to college freshmen. The reactions I get from my students when I tell them my family is from Afghanistan are often hilarious. Some are confused about how an Afghan woman got into a position of authority such as mine. Others start choosing their words all too carefully when discussing issues like the "just war" theory, particularly when it relates to the ethics of U.S. war conduct in Afghanistan or how to define terrorism. In any event, my Afghan nationality carries a newfound influence and adds an element to my interpersonal relations that did not exist before. Once again, I am not judged as an individual but as a representative of Afghanistan and its women. While flattering, at times it seems like a great deal of weight on my shoulders, and I wonder if I will ever be able to lead a life that does not revolve around a consciousness of my being Muslim or Afghan but on my value as just a human being.

But in addition to those mainstream Americans who are suspicious or unsure of Afghans, I have seen anti-war activists protesting in front of the Federal Building in Los Angeles who are clearly not Afghan. I have encountered many focus groups at the university who are trying to reach out to Muslim and Middle Eastern students. Many schools have been offering counseling to help people cope with the stress and difficulties that the attacks on America inflicted. I have found people who are trying to heal our society and become part of a real solution.

❧ ❧

I realize now that the country of my heritage should not be viewed in light of the "failed state" label it has been given by the United Nations. Afghanistan is rich in a history and culture that stretches back five thousand years. Though it is steeped in ancient tradition, it was able to evolve into a modern and peaceful society. If given the chance, care, and attention, it can do so again.

An entire generation of Afghans has grown up with no schooling, no parks or amusement, no laughter or joy, but only sadness, death, and destruction. We might expect this generation to be full of hatred, totally dysfunctional, with no prospects for a bright future. Quite to the contrary, this special generation of Afghans who did not leave their homeland during the war as others did have maintained their identities and have kept hope despite their loss of almost everything that can be lost. They have not resorted to un-Islamic measures of suicide bombings or killing innocent civilians, but rely on God to deliver them from their living hell.

Their faith has paid off, as it always has in the past, and they are on the road to recovery. Hamid Karzai's first task in the interim government implemented in December 2001 was to stabilize Afghanistan and abolish warlordism and hostile foreign forces. Zahir Shah, the former king, returned to Afghanistan in the spring of 2002 for the first time since his exile. A loya jirga convened some weeks later to decide upon the basis for a new government and constitution. By June 2002, the loya jirga elected Karzai to a two-year term as president. It is a hopeful time for people who live in Afghanistan as well as for Afghans who live all over the world.

These new Afghan governments will have many challenges to face, and they will have to prove themselves under the careful scrutiny of the entire world. Afghan-Americans are paying particularly close attention. Many Afghan-Americans fear that the new government is filled with unqualified individuals, and that Karzai is a puppet who has to appease the Northern Alliance, Pakistan, and the U.S. They note that many of the high-ranking officials do not even have high school educations, and others are war criminals and violators of human rights. They perceive that Karzai's Afghan dress is meant to represent the styles of different ethnic groups so that he can be a symbol of unity. However, President Karzai has been quite clear that he is not supporting a puppet regime and emphasizes that he is working during a very strenuous transitional period in the country, so it will take some time to weed out the quirks in the system. In the meantime, the majority Pashtuns feel that the minority Northern Alliance has taken over the country because America has simply generalized and associated all of the Pashtuns with the Taliban.

These strong ethnic tensions continue to bubble, and we have to hope that they will not boil over into more ethnic clashes and desires for retribution. Karzai's new government has been careful to appoint an ethnically balanced cabinet. The factionalization of Afghans under warlords resulted from the war, which led to the emergence of such commanders as protectors. Integrating the diverse groups into a united Afghanistan will be a difficult task.

≈ ≈

The entire international community has suddenly become concerned with Afghanistan's education system, welfare policy, situation with women, and much more. It is a wonderful opportunity for Afghanistan to get the help it needs so direly. It is crucial that the international community, and particularly the United States, play a significant role in the efforts to reconstruct Afghanistan. While some believe that the U.S. should not concern itself with nation building, I think we owe it to the Afghans to help them restore their country. The international community ought to rise to the occasion and finally do right by the Afghans.

U.S. Congressman Dana Rohrabacher of Huntington Beach,

California, has taken a keen interest in Afghanistan and Afghans, dating back to the 1980s—because of gratitude, he says. "The U.S. owes a lot to these people. These were the people who not only defeated the Soviets and brought an end to the Cold War, but also helped us defeat the Taliban." When I asked him about the importance of repairing and rebuilding the relationship between Afghanistan and the United States, he replied, "Understanding the Afghans is vital to our own well-being as Americans. If there's a lesson to be learned, you ignore the Afghans at your own risk." However, he acknowledges that this understanding goes both ways: "Afghans must proclaim themselves Muslim and yet tolerant. Saying that there will be no churches allowed in Afghanistan is just as bad as us saying that we do not want any mosques in our neighborhoods."

Congressman Rohrabacher and Congressman Ed Royce both have been extremely supportive of Afghan-Americans who want to return to Afghanistan to apply their skills and talents to rebuild and improve the country. Mr. Royce was able to include language in the Afghanistan Freedom Support Act, a large aid package, that would make it easier for Afghan-Americans to return and be constructive. Mr. Royce's biggest accomplishment regarding Afghanistan is the reestablishment of Radio Free Afghanistan. After the fall of the Taliban, the primary source of news and information for Afghans was radio, since television had been banned by the Taliban. Radio Free Afghanistan gives Afghans access to world news and communication from Western countries such as the United States.[1]

The tragic events of September 11 have proven even more tragic because they have polarized the world into two opposite camps, the "East" and the "West." In such a short time the globe has quite transparently split apart at the seams, and there seems

---

[1] Information provided by the Office of Congressman Ed Royce, Washington, D.C.

to be no viable way of beginning dialogue and understanding, which is what leads to tolerance and coexistence in this small world. Without dialogue, we are left with the option of more violence. But disparate value systems should not have to mean we live in a divided world.

Afghanistan is only a doorway into this new relationship between the United States and the Islamic world, which will surely evolve over time to include other Muslim countries. Though public interest in Afghanistan's story will eventually fade, the reality is that the same issues and principles will remain as we delve into relationships with those neighboring lands that have similar histories, cultures, and religion.

It is the beginning of a new era, and we will view the world with new eyes. The events of September 11 have left us with an opportunity to probe the principles we operate under, and to challenge our stereotypes and misconceptions of Islam, Muslims, the East, Christians, Jews, America, and the West. For many of us, the pain has left us angry and numb. But after the initial hatred wears off, we are offered the precious chance to give some meaning to the loss of lives and landmarks with the way we react to this monumental situation. After all, it is the only thing we have control over at this stage. We can continue our past behavior and continue to be faced with the same tragic results. Or we can make a conscious decision to change our behavior and seek hope for a renewed future. As a global community, we have an obligation to coexist and an opportunity to work toward understanding and tolerance. If these are genuinely practiced, they will surely lead in only one direction: peace.

EPILOGUE

I f the peoples of the East and West are willing to actually learn about one another's value systems rather than judge them out of hand, they might find common ground to work toward *goals* that are truly universal, rather than ideologies. Such goals can be grounded in our basic human needs and wants.

This process could bind the growing gap between the East and West and unite them with a common purpose. We must begin to heal the growing tensions that have erupted rather than widen the gap, which is after all based only on our cultural differences that are worthy of being celebrated. If we are all working genuinely toward the common goal of coexistence and tolerance, what does it matter how we dress or express our identities and individuality?

Direct dialogue, reaching out so that people can speak for themselves and cutting out secondhand commentators, will help penetrate through layers of stereotypes and lead to the light of understanding. We are being torn between two cultures and pushed into separate camps. We need to learn about each other so we can formulate our common interests. It is imperative that we draw some crucial distinctions between the cultures, politics, and religions of the different peoples of the world. These are entirely separate components that represent the deep, multidimensional nature of our relationship, and they should not be lumped together.

The key to understanding is education. Personal biases aside, education is what sets human beings apart from the rest of creation. I am not referring to formal education in the traditional sense but education itself, pure and simple.

In the case of Afghanistan, which serves as a model for our relationship with Muslim nations, the helpful nations of the international community must not seek to impose their own value systems upon the country. If Afghanistan builds itself as a free society, then it will have the opportunity to openly examine its own values and practices on its own. Other countries that seek to unduly influence Afghanistan's cultural orientation will not only fail to do so but will inflame latent suspicions that foreign powers are once again seeking to interfere in domestic affairs. It will be tempting for nations to try to have their say in such matters, particularly when they are sending financial and diplomatic aid, but we must be true friends and trust the country to act as the sovereign, self-determining nation it is. In the United States, a great deal can be done to help the plight of the Afghans without imposing unwelcome values on them.

Whether we help or not is not a question anymore. We must help Afghanistan because we want to feel safe in the global community, which has become smaller than we had realized. The heat from the fires of Afghanistan can be felt on our doorsteps. We are trying to repair past mistakes and in so doing we must tread carefully. We simply cannot afford to lose this time.

Finally, if we want to successfully combat terrorism, we can either continue on a warpath of escalated destruction, which will eventually lead us to the point of no return, or we can take a step back and realize that the solution does not lie in the might of war or violence but in human understanding, and in the exercise and extension of dialogue that occurs through education and free-flowing exchange. God help us.

INDEX

Photographs in italics

Abrahamic faiths, 77
activism, community, 88, 174
Afghan
    brides, 137
    character, 106
    code of honor, 147
    communists, 59, 106
    community, 31, 69
    gangs, 73
    guests, 147–49
    heritage, 93
    landmarks, 172
    lifestyle, 43
    political factions, 59, 63
    pride, 35
    psyche, 32
    role of women, 119
    weddings, 128
Afghan-American, 66, 174–75
Afghan Freedom Support Act, 185
Afghan Institute of Development, 88
Afghanistan
    arrival in, 7
    first trip to, 2
    restoring of, 173
    returning to, 91
    revisiting, 93
    war in, 50

air strikes, 162, 169
Allah, will of, 161
Al Qaeda, 58, 150, 154
American culture, 165
arous (new bride), 138
Aseel, Maryam Qudrat (author), *108*
Aseel, Samir (husband), *113–14*,
    134–36
attacks, suicide, 155
Aziz Supermarket, 7

bazaar, 2, 12–14
Bible, 157
bin Laden, Osama, 146, 149, 169–71,
    178
burqas, 8, 9, 12, 84–85, 146, 179–80

civil liberties, 67
community activism, 88, 174
Communist, 59
    doctrine, 45, 51
    ideologies, 103–4
    regime, 16–17, 25
    rule, 99
community, Muslim, 87
Concorde exam, 101
conscription, 19
courtships, 126–28

cuisine, Afghan, 6, 20
culture, 33, 38–9, 59, 67, 147

daughters-in-law, 138–39
dowry, 129

education, 33, 100, 103, 184
engagement party, 128
ethnocentrism, 81
expectations, of parents, 42

Farsi-Zubans, 61
freedom fighters, 49, 52, 58

gach, 81, 90
ghaiyrat, 119, 148–49
graduation day, high school, 82
grandparents, 26
Gulf War, 79

Haseena (sister), 85–87, *111*
Hashimi, Rahmatullah, 145–46
Hazaras, 62
Herat, 8
high school graduation, 82
hijab, 79–80, 83–4, 89
homelessness, 97–8
human resouces, 100
Hussein, Saddam, 79

identity, 75
illiteracy, 161
immigrants, 27–31, 90
Islam, 68, 70, 78, 89, 96, 150
    prophets of, 80
    religion of, 122
Islamic
    consciousness, 70
    principles, 39, 89
    values, 104

Jalalabad, 21, 102, *115*
jihad, 154

Kabul, young women of, 3
Kabulis, 6

Kabul University, 2, 3, 102–3, *109*
Kamrany, Mr. and Mrs., *110*
Kamrany, Nake, *110*
Kandahar, 9
Karzai, Hamid (president), 15, 63,
    100, 176, 183–84
Khan, Daoud (former president), 16,
    57
Koh Koh Jan (grandmother), 1, 5, 26,
    111
Koohi-Noor (diamond), 9

Laila (cousin), 3
land mines, 46–47
loya jirga (grand assembly), 95, 183

Marastoon (beggar's house), 98
marriages
    intercultural, 39, 41
    nature of, 125
    proposals of, 125
Masjid Jama'a Herat (mosque), 8
maternal family, of Maryam, *110*
Matthews, Chris, 88
Mazar-e Sharif, 21
media, monitoring of, 179–80
mosques, 21, 120, 141, 166, 181
MSA. *See* Muslim Student Association
Mujadidi, Ezzatullah (teacher),
    141–43
mujahideen, 49–51, 58
mullahs, 83, 121, 161
Muslims, 78, 181
Muslim Student Association (MSA),
    76–77, 86

nationalism, 39, 131
Northern Alliance, 184

Omar (brother), 86–88, *112*
oppression, of women, 124
organizations, humanitarian, 90
Osama bin Laden, 146, 149, 169–71,
    178

pagans, 158
Paghman, 19, *115*
Pakistan, 53
PALM. *See* Physicians Against Land
    Mines
Pashtuns, 61
paternal family, of Maryam, *108*
peace, 186
Physicians Against Land Mines
    (PALM), 46
polygamy, 122–23
Pop Rocks (candy), 10–11
Presidential Palace, *110*
prophets, 157
Psalms, 157
pursuit, concept of, 137–38

Qadeer, Abdul (father), *109*, *112*, *113*
Qudrat, Shaesta (mother), *109*, 117–18
Quran, 9, 51, 68, 75, 82, 121, 144, 157

Radio Free Afghanistan, 185
Ramadan, 75
reception, 129
Red Army, 22, 51, 57, 166
refugee camps, 55
refugees, 1, 27–30, 64, 73, 107
reputation, 34, 40
resistance forces, 166
Rohrabacher, Dana (congressman),
    184, 185
royal garden, *115*
Royce, Ed (congressman), 185
rugs, Afghan, 11

salad bowl cultures, 38, 59, 67
self-esteem, 123
September 11th, 66, 86–88, 96, 178,
    181–82, 185–86
shirni (candy), 127
shura (parliment), 95
smugglers, 19, 53–54

Soviet
    atrocities, 46
    doctrine, 105
    invasion, 26, 29, 38, 48, 56, 96, 120,
        131
    occupation, 46
    scholarships, 103
Soviet Union
    alliance of, 16–18
    studying in, 4
statues, Bamiyan Buddhist, 149–50
stereotypes, 81, 121, 124, 162
suitors, 132–34

Taliban, 63, 120, 145–47, 150–53, 165
Taraki, government of, 16–18
teachers, 141–43
terrorism, 156
Torah, 157
traditions, 33, 42, 71–3, *114*, 130, 139
trauma, psychological, 173
tribalism, 60

University of Southern California
    (UCLA), 65

Valls, Andrew (philosopher), 156
value systems, 68, 121, 174, 187–88
virginity, 71

warfare, Islamic principles of, 156
wedding
    ceremony, *114*, 129
    Maryam and Samir, *113*, *114*
    of parents, 5, 6, *110*
    plans for, 136
womanhood, ascending to, 125
women, treatment of, 120, 179
work ethic, 27
World Trade Center, 169, 172, 177

Zahir Shah (king), 94–97, 104, 152,
    183